The Maths Handbook

a reference for secondary students

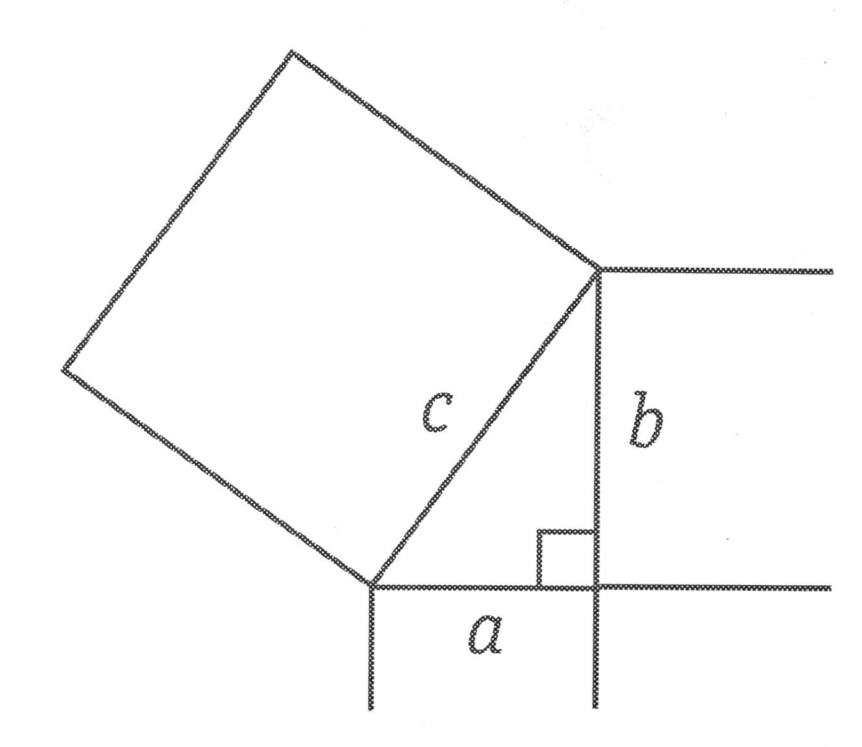

The Maths Handbook

a reference for secondary students

maths facts
definitions
formulas
theorems
terminology

PHOENIX EDUCATION

George Fisher

For Daniele and Jacqui

First Published in 1995
Second edition published in 1998
Reprinted 1999, 2001, 2004, 2006

Phoenix Education Pty Ltd
PO Box 197
Albert Park 3206
Australia

Copyright © George Fisher 1995, 1998

All rights reserved. Apart from any fair dealing for the purposes of study, research, criticism of review as permitted under the copyright act, no part of this book may be reproduced by any process without permission. Copyright owners may take legal action against a person or organisation who infringes their copyright through unauthorised copying. Inquiries should be directed to the publisher.

ISBN 1 875695 87 7

Cover design by Sarn Potter

Design and page make-up by Mathematical Desktop Publishing

Printed in Australia by Shannon Books

Contents

About this book ... vii

Chapter 1	Number	1
2	Algebra	16
3	Geometry	28
4	Measurement	49
5	Statistics	56
6	Probability	66
7	Consumer arithmetic	69
8	Trigonometry	73
9	Coordinate geometry	79
10	Functions and mapping	86
11	Theory of logarithms	92
12	Polynomials	95
13	Matrices and transformations	100
14	Surveying	106
15	Navigation	115
16	Linear programming	123
17	Set theory	125

Index ... 128

About this book

This is a reference book for all secondary maths students. You can use it at school or at home, and will find it particularly useful for homework and revision.

Use this book to
- check how to do something
- look up forgotten facts
- check on a formula, theorem or definition
- study or revise a topic

The book is divided into seventeen mathematics areas and the information is broken into short, clear explanations and definitions. Each concept is demonstrated by worked examples to show how it is applied in practice.

You can look up
- maths facts
- definitions
- theorems
- formulas
- procedures and methods
- terminology

Keep this book with your maths folder and refer to it whenever you need. Use the table of contents if you want to read about or revise a whole topic. If you want to look up a specific fact or concept, use the **index** at the back of the book.

Chapter 1
NUMBER

Numbers and digits

Roman and Hindu–Arabic numerals

I	1	XC	90
II	2	C	100
III	3	CC	200
IV	4	CCC	300
V	5	CD	400
VI	6	D	500
VII	7	DC	600
VIII	8	DCC	700
IX	9	DCCC	800
X	10	CM	900
XX	20	M	1000
XXX	30	$\overline{V}$	5 000
XL	40	$\overline{X}$	10 000
L	50	$\overline{L}$	50 000
LX	60	$\overline{C}$	100 000
LXX	70	$\overline{D}$	500 000
LXXX	80	$\overline{M}$	1 000 000

Example: 1998 = MCMXCVIII

Place value

The value of each digit in a number depends on its **place** in that number.

Millions	Hundred thousands	Ten thousands	Thousands	Hundreds	Tens	Units
1 000 000	100 000	10 000	1000	100	10	1
10^6	10^5	10^4	10^3	10^2	10^1	1
			6	5	3	8
3	2	4	1	6	0	8

Examples:

6538 = six thousand, five hundred and thirty-eight

3 241 608 = 3 million, two hundred and forty-one thousand, six hundred and eight

In the number 436 the value of the digit 3 is 30.

In the number 346 the value of the digit 3 is 300.

In the number 3 241 608 the value of the digit 3 is 3 000 000.

Expanded notation

In expanded notation a number is written as the sum of each digit multiplied by its place value.

Example:
$$6538 = (6 \times 1000) + (5 \times 100) + (3 \times 10) + (8 \times 1)$$

Order of operations

1. ( ) Do operations within grouping symbols.
2. ×; ÷ Do multiplications and divisions as they appear (from left to right).
3. +; − Do additions and subtractions as they appear (from left to right).

Examples:

$$\begin{aligned} 23 - 12 + 5 - 2 \\ = 11 + 5 - 2 \\ = 16 - 2 \\ = 14 \end{aligned} \qquad \begin{aligned} 45 \div 5 \times 7 + 3 \\ = 9 \times 7 + 3 \\ = 63 + 3 \\ = 21 \end{aligned} \qquad \begin{aligned} 3(5 + 7) \\ = 3 \times 12 \\ = 36 \end{aligned}$$

Number properties

1. Multiplying any number by 1 leaves it unchanged.	$578 \times 1 = 578$
2. Multiplying any number by 0 gives the answer zero.	$578 \times 0 = 0$
3. Adding 0 to any number leaves it unchanged.	$578 + 0 = 578$
4. When adding two numbers the order does not change the answer.	$23 + 16 = 16 + 23$

5. When multiplying two numbers the order does not change the answer.	$23 \times 16 = 16 \times 23$
6. When adding two or more numbers, we can add them in any order.	$32 + 59 + 28 = (32 + 28) + 59$ $= 60 + 59$ $= 119$
7. When multiplying more than two numbers, we can multiply them in any order.	$4 \times 25 \times 37 = (4 \times 25) \times 37$ or $4 \times (25 \times 37) = 3700$ (The first is easier.)

Language

The result of *addition* is the *sum*.
The result of *subtraction* is the *difference*.
The result of *multiplication* is the *product*.
The result of *division* is the *quotient*.

Symbols

$+$	plus
$-$	minus
$\times$	times
$\div$	divided by
$=$	equals
$\neq$	is not equal to
$\approx$	is approximately equal to
$<$	is less than
$>$	is greater than
$\leq$	is less than or equal to
$\geq$	is greater than or equal to
$\sqrt{}$	the square root of
$\sqrt[3]{}$	the cube root of
5^2	five squared
∞	infinity
$\propto$	is proportional to
$\equiv$	is equivalent to, or congruent
$\therefore$	therefore
$\because$	because
e.g.	for example
i.e.	that is
%	percentage
Σ	the sum of
$\Rightarrow$	implies

Directed numbers

These are numbers that have signs, positive or negative, to indicate the position of the number relative to zero on the number line. Positive numbers are to the right and negative numbers are to the left.

Positions on the number line

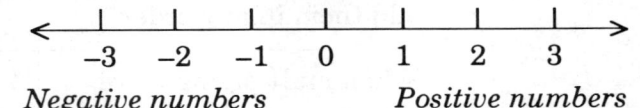

$$\leftarrow \;|\;\;\;|\;\;\;|\;\;\;|\;\;\;|\;\;\;|\;\;\;| \rightarrow$$
$$-3\;\;-2\;\;-1\;\;\;0\;\;\;1\;\;\;2\;\;\;3$$

Negative numbers *Positive numbers*

Operations

These are processes carrying out the rules of procedure such as addition, subtraction, multiplication, division.

Examples:

$-8 + 5 = -3$ $-8 + (-5) = -13$

$-8 - 5 = -13$ $-8 - (-5) = -3$

$-8 \times (-5) = 40$ $-8 + (-4) = 2$

Decimals, fractions and percentages

Fractions, decimals and percentages are different ways of showing the same idea.

Fractions

❏ A fraction is a quotient of two quantities. The dividend is called the numerator and the divisor the denominator.
A **simple fraction** is a fraction whose numerator and denominator are both integers.

$$\frac{a}{b} \;\;\begin{matrix}\leftarrow \text{numerator}\\ \leftarrow \text{denominator}\end{matrix}$$

❏ Fractions whose numerator is smaller than the denominator are called **proper fractions**, e.g., $\frac{2}{3}$.

❏ Fractions whose numerator is larger than the denominator are called **improper fractions**, e.g., $\frac{7}{3}$.

❏ Any improper fraction can be converted to a **mixed number**, which is the sum of a whole number and a proper fraction.

Example: $\frac{7}{3} = 2\frac{1}{3}$

Equivalent fractions

These are fractions which have the same value.
$$\frac{3}{4} = \frac{6}{8} = \frac{15}{20} = \frac{21}{28} = \text{etc.}$$

Lowest common denominator (LCD)

This is the lowest counting number divisible by each of the denominators, that is, the lowest common multiple of all the denominators, e.g., $\frac{3}{5}, \frac{5}{8}$ LCD = 40.

Adding and subtracting fractions

Fractions that have the same denominator are called *like fractions*, while fractions which have different denominators are called *unlike fractions*.

When adding or subtracting fractions, change them to equivalent fractions with the same denominator using the **LCD**.

Examples:

$$\frac{3}{7} + \frac{2}{5} = \frac{3}{7} \times \frac{5}{5} + \frac{2}{5} \times \frac{7}{7} \qquad \frac{5}{6} - \frac{5}{8} = \frac{5}{6} \times \frac{4}{4} - \frac{5}{8} \times \frac{3}{3}$$

$$= \frac{15}{35} + \frac{14}{35} \qquad\qquad\qquad = \frac{20}{24} - \frac{15}{24}$$

$$= \frac{29}{35} \qquad\qquad\qquad\qquad = \frac{5}{24}$$

Adding and subtracting mixed numbers

Add or subtract the whole numbers, then add or subtract the fraction parts. (Take care with signs.)

Examples:
$$3\frac{2}{3} + 1\frac{1}{7} = 3 + 1 + \frac{2}{3} + \frac{1}{7}$$

$$= 4 + \frac{2}{3} \times \frac{7}{7} + \frac{1}{7} \times \frac{3}{3}$$

$$= 4 + \frac{14 + 3}{21}$$

$$= 4\frac{17}{21}$$

$$7\frac{2}{3} - 4\frac{1}{4} = 7 - 4 + \frac{2}{3} - \frac{1}{4}$$

$$= 3 + \frac{2}{3} \times \frac{4}{4} - \frac{1}{4} \times \frac{3}{3}$$

$$= 3 + \frac{8-3}{12}$$

$$= 3\frac{5}{12}$$

$$7\frac{2}{3} - 4\frac{5}{6} = 7 - 4 + \frac{2}{3} - \frac{5}{6}$$

$$= 3 + \frac{2}{3} \times \frac{2}{2} - \frac{5}{6}$$

$$= 3 + \frac{4-5}{6}$$

$$= 3 - \frac{1}{6}$$

$$= 2\frac{5}{6}$$

Multiplying and dividing fractions

Multiply the numerators and multiply the denominators:

$$\frac{3}{7} \times \frac{2}{5} = \frac{3 \times 2}{7 \times 5} = \frac{6}{35}$$

Cancel common factors from both numerator and denominator, leaving an easier product:

$$\frac{{}^1\cancel{5}}{{}_4\cancel{8}} \times \frac{\cancel{6}^{\,3}}{\cancel{25}_{\,5}} = \frac{1}{4} \times \frac{3}{5} = \frac{3}{20}$$

For division, the divisor is turned upside down and then the fractions are multiplied:

$$\frac{3}{7} \div \frac{2}{5} = \frac{3}{7} \times \frac{5}{2} = \frac{3 \times 5}{7 \times 2} = \frac{15}{14}$$

Multiplying and dividing mixed numbers

Change the mixed numbers to improper fractions and then multiply or divide as for fractions.

Examples:

$$5\frac{1}{2} \times 3\frac{3}{4} = \frac{11}{2} \times \frac{15}{4}$$
$$= \frac{165}{8}$$
$$= 20\frac{5}{8}$$

$$3\frac{5}{8} \div 2\frac{1}{3} = \frac{29}{8} \div \frac{7}{3}$$
$$= \frac{29}{8} \times \frac{3}{7}$$
$$= \frac{87}{56}$$
$$= 1\frac{31}{56}$$

Decimals

A decimal is a fraction whose denominator is a power of 10. For example, 4·638 can be written in expanded notation using:

Units		Tenths	Hundredths	Thousandths
4	•	6	3	8

$$= (4 \times 1) + \left(6 \times \frac{1}{10}\right) + \left(3 \times \frac{1}{100}\right) + \left(8 \times \frac{1}{1000}\right)$$

Adding and subtracting decimals

$$\begin{array}{r} 12\cdot378 \\ +9\cdot08 \\ \hline 21\cdot458 \end{array} \qquad \begin{array}{r} 12\cdot378 \\ -9\cdot08 \\ \hline 3\cdot298 \end{array}$$

Always align the decimal points.

Multiplying and dividing decimals

When multiplying, the answer has the total number of decimal places that each of the factors contains.

$$12\cdot7 \times 0\cdot4 = 5\cdot08$$

When dividing, move the decimal points to the right to make the divisor a whole number.

$$12\cdot7 \div 0\cdot4 = 127 \div 4 = 31\cdot75$$

Rounding

Writing an answer to a given degree of accuracy:

4·348 = 4·35 correct to two decimal places

4·348 = 4·3 correct to one decimal place

Writing an answer to a given number of significant figures:

6831 = 7000 simplified to one significant figure

5·732 14 = 5·7 simplified to two significant figures

Percentages

A percentage is a fraction with a denominator of one hundred.

Example: $\qquad 25\% = \dfrac{25}{100} = \dfrac{1}{4}$

Conversions

$$37\% = \frac{37}{100} = 0{\cdot}37 \qquad \frac{5}{8} = 0{\cdot}625 = 62{\cdot}5\%$$

Fraction	Decimal	Percentage
$\frac{1}{2}$	0·5	50%
$\frac{1}{3}$	0·333 333 3 …	$33\frac{1}{3}\%$
$\frac{2}{3}$	0·666 666 6 …	$66\frac{2}{3}\%$
$\frac{1}{4}$	0·25	25%
$\frac{3}{4}$	0·75	75%
$\frac{1}{5}$	0·2	20%
$\frac{2}{5}$	0·4	40%
$\frac{3}{5}$	0·6	60%
$\frac{4}{5}$	0·8	80%
$\frac{1}{6}$	0·166 666 6 …	$16\frac{2}{3}\%$
$\frac{5}{6}$	0·833 333 3 …	$83\frac{1}{3}\%$
$\frac{1}{8}$	0·125	12·5%
$\frac{3}{8}$	0·375	37·5%
$\frac{5}{8}$	0·625	62·5%
$\frac{7}{8}$	0·875	87·5%
$\frac{1}{10}$	0·1	10%
$\frac{3}{10}$	0·3	30%
$\frac{7}{10}$	0·7	70%
$\frac{9}{10}$	0·9	90%

Percentage composition

Convert the percentage to a decimal or a fraction.

Examples: 35% of 560 = 0·35 × 560
  = 196

$$35 \text{ out of } 40 = \frac{35}{40} \times 100\%$$
$$= 87{\cdot}5\%$$

Number theory

Counting (or natural) numbers
That is, $\{1, 2, 3, 4, 5, ...\}$

Cardinal numbers
A number which designates how many things.
That is, $\{0, 1, 2, 3, 4, ...\}$
Example: In *4 apples* the 4 is a cardinal number.

Ordinal numbers
A number which denotes position. That is, 1st, 2nd, etc.

Integers
The set of positive and negative **whole numbers** as well as zero is called the set of integers.
That is, $\{...-4, -3, -2, -1, 0, 1, 2, 3, 4, ...\}$

Odd and even numbers
Even numbers are divisible by 2: $\{2, 4, 6, 8, 10, ...\}$

Odd numbers leave a remainder of 1 after division by 2: $\{1, 3, 5, 7, 9, 11, ...\}$

Square numbers
Square numbers can be represented by dots in the shape of a square.

Example:

    1   4   9   16

Triangular numbers
Triangular numbers can be represented by dots in the shape of a triangle.

Example:

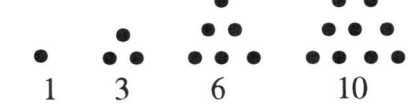

    1   3   6   10

Factors and multiples
A **factor** is a whole number that can be divided exactly into another number.

A **multiple** of a given number is any number into which that number will divide exactly.

From the number sentence, $9 \times 7 = 63$, the following true statements can be made:

>63 is the product of 9 and 7
>9 is a factor of 63
>7 is a factor of 63
>63 is a multiple of 9
>63 is a multiple of 7

A **common factor** is a factor that is shared by two or more numbers. For example, 7 is a common factor of 14 and 63.

Primes and composites

- ❏ A prime number has exactly two elements in its set of factors, 1 and itself.
- ❏ A composite number has more than two elements in its set of factors.
- ❏ The number 1 has only one element in its set of factors, therefore it is neither prime nor composite.
- ❏ The set of primes is $\{2, 3, 5, 7, 11, 13, 17, 19, 23, ...\}$.

Prime factors

A prime number that divides exactly into a given number is one of its prime factors, for example, 2, 3 and 7 are prime factors of 42.

Example: The prime factors of 108.

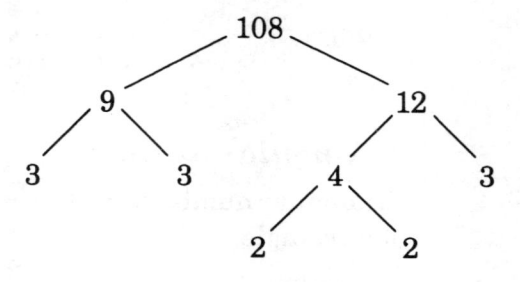

```
            108
           /    \
          9      12
         / \    /  \
        3   3  4    3
              / \
             2   2
```

$$108 = 3 \times 3 \times 2 \times 2 \times 3$$
$$= 3^3 \times 2^2$$

Highest common factor (HCF)

The highest common factor of two numbers is the largest number that divides both numbers.

HCF by prime factors

For example, the HCF of 48 and 72:

$48 = 2 \times 2 \times 2 \times 2 \times 3 \qquad 72 = 2 \times 2 \times 2 \times 3 \times 3$

HCF is obtained by multiplying all the common factors, that is, HCF is $2 \times 2 \times 2 \times 3 = 24$.

Lowest common multiple (LCM)

The lowest common multiple of two numbers is the smallest number that is exactly divisible by each of the two numbers.

LCM by prime factors

For example, the LCM of 48 and 72:

$48 = 2 \times 2 \times 2 \times 2 \times 3 \qquad 72 = 2 \times 2 \times 2 \times 3 \times 3$

Take the highest number of prime factors from each number and multiply to get the lowest common multiple, that is,

LCM is $2 \times 2 \times 2 \times 2 \times 3 \times 3 = 144$.

Square and cube roots

The **square root** of a number is a number which when multiplied by itself produces the given number.

The **cube root** of a number is a number whose cube is the given number.

$\sqrt{..}$ means 'the square root of'.

Example: $\sqrt{25} = 5$ since $5^2 = 25$

$\sqrt[3]{..}$ means 'the cube root of'.

Example: $\sqrt[3]{64} = 4$ since $4^3 = 64$

Divisibility tests

Divisor	Divisibility test
2	The number must be even, that is, it must end in 0, 2, 4, 6, or 8. *Example:* 4536 is divisible by 2
3	The sum of the digits must be divisible by 3. *Example:* 4371 is divisible by 3 since $4 + 3 + 7 + 1 = 15$, which is divisible by 3.
4	The number formed by the last two digits must be divisible by 4. *Example:* 57 148 is divisible by 4 since 48 is divisible by 4.

5	The last digit must be 5 or 0. *Example*: 36 815 is divisible by 5	
6	The number must be even and the sum of its digits must be divisible by 3. *Example*: 31 476 is divisible by 6	
8	The number formed by the last three digits must be divisible by 8. *Example*: 571 248 is divisible by 8 since 248 is divisible by 8.	
9	The sum of the digits must be divisible by 9. *Example*: 4671 is divisible by 9 since $4 + 6 + 7 + 1 = 18$, which is divisible by 9.	
10	The last digit must be 0. *Example*: 4370 is divisible by 10	
11	The sum of the odd digits and the sum of the even digits must differ by 0 or a multiple of 11. *Example*: 6 493 718 is divisible by 11 since $(6 + 9 + 7 + 8) - (4 + 3 + 1) = 22$, which is divisible by 11.	
25	The last two digits must be 00, 25, 50, or 75. *Example*: 67 025 is divisible by 25	

Rational and irrational numbers

Rational numbers

A rational number is one that can be expressed in the form of a fraction $\frac{p}{q}$, where p and q have no common factors and $q \neq 0$.

Examples:

- Fractions: $\frac{7}{8}$
- Terminating decimals: $0 \cdot 45 = \frac{45}{100} = \frac{9}{20}$
- Recurring decimals: $0 \cdot \dot{1}\dot{3} = \frac{13}{99}$

  That is, $1 \times 0 \cdot \dot{1}\dot{3} = 0 \cdot \dot{1}\dot{3}$

  $100 \times 0 \cdot \dot{1}\dot{3} = 13 \cdot \dot{1}\dot{3}$

  $99 \times 0 \cdot \dot{1}\dot{3} = 13$

  $0 \cdot \dot{1}\dot{3} = \frac{13}{99}$

Irrational numbers

An irrational number cannot be expressed as a fraction.

Examples:

Surds: $\sqrt{5}$ $\sqrt{5} = 2{\cdot}236\,0067\,977\,...$

Non-terminating and *non-recurring decimals*, such as π which is the ratio of the circumference to the diameter of a circle.

$$\pi = 3{\cdot}14159\,...\quad (\pi \text{ has been calculated to over } 100\,000 \text{ decimal places.})$$

Ratio

A ratio is a comparison of two or more quantities of the *same type* in a definite order.

The ratio can be written in the form $a:b$ and has the value $\dfrac{a}{b}$

Example: What is the ratio of $2 to 50c?

Since the units are different, first express them in the same units, that is, $2 = 200 c. The ratio is $200:50$, which simplifies to $4:1$.

Equivalent ratios

They have the same value. Ratios are simplified and manipulated like fractions.

Example: $3:2 = 6:4 = 30:20 = 63:42$, etc.

Division of quantities into ratios

Example:

Two businessmen divide up their profits according to their investment. John invested $30 000 and Bill invested $25 000. How should they divide up profits of $8800?

The ratio is $30\,000:25\,000$, which simplifies to $6:5$ representing 11 parts, of which John gets 6 parts and Bill gets 5 parts.

$$\text{John gets } \frac{6}{11} \times \$8800 = \$4800.$$

$$\text{Bill gets } \frac{5}{11} \times \$8800 = \$4000.$$

Scale drawing

A scale drawing of an object is the same shape as the original object but of different size. The relationship is shown as a ratio.

Scale = length of drawing : length of object.

A map scale can be written in one of two ways:

1 mm : 1 km   or   1 : 1 000 000

This means that a length of 1 mm on the drawing represents a distance of 1 km in reality.

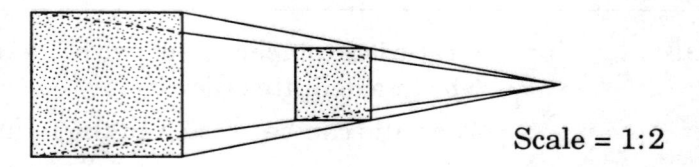

Scale = 1:2

Rates

A rate is a comparison of two quantities of *different type*. It is expressed by writing down how many of the first quantity correspond to *one* of the second.

Example: 300 kilometres in 4 hours = 75 km per hour
= 75 km/h

One of the most common uses of rates connects distance(D), speed(S), and time(T).

$$D = S \times T \qquad S = \frac{D}{T} \qquad T = \frac{D}{S}$$

By covering the quantity you want, this triangle will show you what to do.

Conversions

Example:
Convert 72 kilometres per hour to metres per second.
Since 1 km = 1000 m, we multiply by 1000,
and 1 h = 3600 s, we divide by 3600.

$$72 \text{ km/h} = 72 \times \frac{1000}{3600}$$
$$= 20 \text{ m/s}$$

Scientific notation

Very large and very small numbers are more easily expressed using powers of 10.

$$590\,000\,000 = 5 \cdot 9 \times 10^8$$
$$0 \cdot 000\,006 = 6 \times 10^{-6}$$

[handwritten: 59×6^7]

Jump the decimal point forwards or backwards to give a number between 1 and 10. Use the number of jumps as the power (⁺ve to the right, ⁻ve to the left).

Chapter 2
ALGEBRA

This is a branch of mathematics that studies number systems and number properties, using symbols or letters to stand for the unknown values.

Introductory algebra

Pronumerals

A **pronumeral** takes the place of a *numeral*. The most commonly used pronumerals are letters, especially lower-case letters, for example a, b, x, y.

Pronumerals can be replaced by specific number values.

Some pronumerals are referred to as *variables*.

In $y = 3x + 2$ both x and y are variables.

x is the *independent variable*, as its value is chosen at random. y is the *dependent variable*, as its value depends on the value of x chosen.

Some pronumerals are referred to as *constants*.

In $y = mx + c$ both m and c are arbitrary constants, as they can be replaced by numbers to leave the expression in terms of x and y.

Examples: $y = 5x + 3$, $y = -3x + 7$

Substitution

This is the replacement of a pronumeral by a number.

If $x = 5, y = 3, z = -2$, then $x \times y + z = 5 \times 3 + (-2)$
$$= 13$$

Examples:

❏ Find $t^4 - t^2 + 1$ if $t = 2\sqrt{3}$.

$$t^4 - t^2 + 1 = \left(2\sqrt{3}\right)^4 - \left(2\sqrt{3}\right)^2 + 1$$
$$= 16 \times 9 - 4 \times 3 + 1$$
$$= 133$$

- Find $A^4 B$ if $A = \left(\dfrac{2}{3}\right)^2$ and $B = \left(\dfrac{3}{4}\right)^2$.

$$A^4 B = \left[\left(\dfrac{2}{3}\right)^2\right]^4 \cdot \left[\left(\dfrac{3}{4}\right)^2\right]$$

$$= \dfrac{2^8}{3^8} \times \dfrac{3^2}{2^4} = \dfrac{2^4}{3^6} = \dfrac{16}{729}$$

Algebraic abbreviations

$a \times b$ can be written as ab, that is, ab means a times b.

$5xy$ means 5 times x times y

$n \times 7$ is written as $7n$, not $n7$

The number written before a pronumeral is called the *coefficient*. For example, in $5m$, 5 is the coefficient of m; $a + b$ can only be written in another form as $b + a$.

Like and unlike terms

In algebra, expressions are called **like terms** if they have the same pronumeral and power.

Like terms can be added and subtracted. Unlike terms do not contain the same pronumeral or power. Unlike terms cannot be added or subtracted.

Examples:
- $5x$ and $3x$ are like terms
- $3mn^2$ and $-8mn^2$ are like terms
- $4a$ and $9b$ are unlike terms

Simplifying algebraic expressions

Algebraic expressions can be simplified by collecting like terms.

Examples:
- $12m + 5m = 17m$
- $3x + 6y + 7x - 2y$

$\quad = 3x + 7x + 6y - 2y \quad$ (collecting like terms)

$\quad = 10x + 4y$

Note that the plus or the minus sign *always* belongs to the term following the sign.

Removing grouping symbols

$$a(b+c) = ab+ac \qquad a(b-c) = ab-ac$$

Examples:
$$3(x+5) = 3x+15$$
$$-5(m-7) = -5m+35$$
$$3x(5+2x) = 15x+6x^2$$

Binomial products

Each term in every bracket is multiplied by each term in every other bracket.

Examples:
$$(a+b)(c+d) = ac+ad+bc+bd$$
$$(x+2)(x+5) = x^2+7x+10$$

Perfect squares

To square a binomial, we square the first term, then add twice the product of the two terms, then add the square of the second term.

Examples:
$$(a+b)^2 = a^2+2ab+b^2$$
$$(x+3)^2 = x^2+6x+9$$

Factorising

Common factors

Example: $3x^2-9x = 3x \times x - 3x \times 3 = 3x(x-3)$

This *reverses* the removal of the brackets.

Difference of two squares

$$A^2-B^2 = (A-B)(A+B)$$

Example:
$$4x^2-25y^2 = (2x)^2-(5y)^2$$
$$= (2x-5y)(2x+5y)$$

Trinomials

Monic (coefficient of x^2 is 1)

Example:
$$x^2+8x+15 = (x+\ )(x+\ )$$
$$x^2-8x+15 = (x-\ )(x-\ )$$

indicates the signs in the brackets

indicates that signs in brackets are the same

these numbers are found using product and sum, i.e. product of 15 and sum of 8

$$\therefore\ x^2+8x+15 = (x+5)(x+3)$$
$$x^2-8x+15 = (x-5)(x-3)$$

Example: $\quad x^2+2x-15 = (x+\ )(x-\ )$
$\qquad\qquad x^2-2x-15 = (x-\ )(x+\ )$

- indicates the sign of the larger numeral
- indicates that signs in brackets are different
- these numbers are found using product and difference, i.e. product of 15 and difference of 2

$$\therefore\ x^2+2x-15 = (x+5)(x-3)$$
$$x^2-2x-15 = (x-5)(x+3)$$

Non-monic (coefficient of x^2 is not 1)

Example: $\quad 3x^2+2x-16 = \dfrac{(3x\ \ )(3x\ \ )}{3}$

Multiply 3 and $-16 \Rightarrow -48$
and use the product and difference as before,
i.e. $\ 8\times 6 = 48\ $ and $\ 8-6 = 2$

$$\therefore\ 3x^2+2x-16 = \dfrac{(3x+8)(3x-6)}{3}$$

Factorise $3x-6$

$$3x^2+2x-16 = \dfrac{(3x+8)\,3(x-2)}{3}$$
$$= (3x+8)(x-2)$$

Perfect squares

$$A^2+2AB+B^2 = (A+B)^2$$
$$A^2-2AB+B^2 = (A-B)^2$$

Examples: $\quad x^2+20x+100 = (x+10)^2$
$\qquad\qquad x^2-12x+36 = (x-6)^2$

Grouping terms

Examples: $\quad ax+by-bx-ay = ax-bx-ay+by$
$\qquad\qquad\qquad\qquad\ = x(a-b)-y(a-b)$
$\qquad\qquad\qquad\qquad\ = (a-b)(x-y)$

$$x^3+x^2+x+1 = x^2(x+1)+1(x+1)$$
$$= (x+1)(x^2+1)$$

Algebraic fractions

Reduction

Example: $$\frac{x^2 - 8x + 15}{x - 5} = \frac{(x-3)(x-5)}{x-5}$$
$$= x - 3$$

Multiplication and division

Example: $$\frac{x+3}{x-2} \times \frac{x^2 - 4}{2x} \div \frac{x^2 - 9}{x}$$
$$= \frac{x+3}{x-2} \times \frac{(x+2)(x-2)}{2x} \times \frac{x}{(x+3)(x-3)}$$
$$= \frac{x+2}{2(x-3)}$$

Addition and subtraction

Example: $$\frac{m+n}{2} + \frac{2m-n}{3} - \frac{m+3n}{6}$$
$$= \frac{3(m+n) + 2(2m-n) - (m+3n)}{6}$$
$$= \frac{3m + 3n + 4m - 2n - m - 3n}{6}$$
$$= \frac{6m - 2n}{6} = \frac{2(3m-n)}{6}$$
$$= \frac{3m - n}{3}$$

Quadratic surds

A **surd** is an expression involving unresolved *roots* of numbers. Thus surds are irrational numbers. A square root is called a quadratic surd, a cube root is called a cubic surd, etc.

Examples:

$\sqrt{2}$ is a surd, $\sqrt{3}$ is a surd,

$\sqrt{9}$ is *not* a surd because $\sqrt{9} = 3$, which is resolved.

Laws of surds

1. $\sqrt{a} \times \sqrt{b} = \sqrt{ab}$ Example: $\sqrt{5} \times \sqrt{3} = \sqrt{15}$

2. $\dfrac{\sqrt{a}}{\sqrt{b}} = \sqrt{\dfrac{a}{b}}$ Example: $\dfrac{\sqrt{21}}{\sqrt{3}} = \sqrt{7}$

3. $(\sqrt{a})^2 = a$ Example: $(\sqrt{5})^2 = 5$

4. $\sqrt{a^2 b} = a\sqrt{b}$ Example: $\sqrt{50} = \sqrt{25} \times \sqrt{2}$
$= 5\sqrt{2}$

5. $a\sqrt{c} + b\sqrt{c} = (a+b)\sqrt{c}$
   Examples: $7\sqrt{3} + 2\sqrt{3} = 9\sqrt{3}$
   $7\sqrt{3} - 2\sqrt{3} = 5\sqrt{3}$
   $\sqrt{128} + \sqrt{32} = 8\sqrt{2} + 4\sqrt{2} = 12\sqrt{2}$

6. $a\sqrt{c} \times b\sqrt{d} = ab\sqrt{cd}$
   Example: $7\sqrt{3} \times 5\sqrt{2} = 35\sqrt{6}$

7. If a, b, c, d are rational numbers, and $a + \sqrt{b} = c + \sqrt{d}$, then $a = c$ and $b = d$ if $\sqrt{b}$ and $\sqrt{d}$ are irrational.

Rationalising the denominator

This is the removal of the radical from the denominator by multiplying numerator and denominator by the same radical quantity.

1. $\dfrac{1}{\sqrt{a}} = \dfrac{1}{\sqrt{a}} \times \dfrac{\sqrt{a}}{\sqrt{a}} = \dfrac{\sqrt{a}}{a}$

   Example: $\dfrac{1}{\sqrt{3}} = \dfrac{1}{\sqrt{3}} \times \dfrac{\sqrt{3}}{\sqrt{3}} = \dfrac{\sqrt{3}}{3}$

2. $\dfrac{1}{a\sqrt{b}} = \dfrac{1}{a\sqrt{b}} \times \dfrac{\sqrt{b}}{\sqrt{b}} = \dfrac{\sqrt{b}}{ab}$

   Example: $\dfrac{1}{2\sqrt{3}} = \dfrac{1}{2\sqrt{3}} \times \dfrac{\sqrt{3}}{\sqrt{3}} = \dfrac{\sqrt{3}}{6}$

3. $\dfrac{1}{\sqrt{a}+\sqrt{b}} = \dfrac{1}{\sqrt{a}+\sqrt{b}} \times \dfrac{\sqrt{a}-\sqrt{b}}{\sqrt{a}-\sqrt{b}} = \dfrac{\sqrt{a}-\sqrt{b}}{a-b}$

   Example: $\dfrac{1}{\sqrt{5}+\sqrt{2}} = \dfrac{1}{\sqrt{5}+\sqrt{2}} \times \dfrac{\sqrt{5}-\sqrt{2}}{\sqrt{5}-\sqrt{2}}$

   $= \dfrac{\sqrt{5}-\sqrt{2}}{3}$

4. $\dfrac{1}{a\sqrt{b}-\sqrt{c}} = \dfrac{1}{a\sqrt{b}-\sqrt{c}} \times \dfrac{a\sqrt{b}+\sqrt{c}}{a\sqrt{b}+\sqrt{c}} = \dfrac{a\sqrt{b}+\sqrt{c}}{a^2b-c}$

Example: $\dfrac{1}{3\sqrt{5}-\sqrt{2}} = \dfrac{1}{3\sqrt{5}-\sqrt{2}} \times \dfrac{3\sqrt{5}+\sqrt{2}}{3\sqrt{5}+\sqrt{2}}$

$= \dfrac{3\sqrt{5}+\sqrt{2}}{43}$

Conjugates

Conjugates are two binomial expressions containing the same terms between them.

Example: $2a+3b$ and $2a-3b$ are conjugates

$\sqrt{3}-\sqrt{2}$ and $\sqrt{3}+\sqrt{2}$ are conjugates

In 3 and 4 above, we need to multiply the numerator and denominator of the fraction by the conjugate of the denominator.

Indices

Defining indices

When *adding* the same quantity several times we use **multiplication** as a shortcut.

Example: $a+a+a+a+a+a+a = 7a$

When *multiplying* the same quantity several times we use **indices** as a shortcut.

Example: $a \times a \times a \times a \times a \times a \times a = a^7$

7 is an **index** to indicate the number of factors of a.

Example: $5 \times m \times m \times m \times 4 \times p = 20m^3p$

Note that the index 3 belongs only to m and not to p.

Multiplication

When multiplying terms together, **add** the indices of the like pronumerals.

Examples: $a^7 \times a^2 = (a \times a \times a \times a \times a \times a \times a) \times (a \times a) = a^9$

$7m^5 \times 5m^4 = 35m^9$

$a^7 \times a = a^8$ (*Note* that $a = a^1$)

ALGEBRA

Division

When *dividing* terms, **subtract** the indices of the like pronumerals.

Examples: $a^7 \div a^2 = (a \times a \times a \times a \times a \times a \times a) \div (a \times a) = a^5$

$20m^5 \div 5m^4 = 4m$

$a^7 \div a = a^6$ (*Note* that $a = a^1$)

Powers of indices

For expressions like $(a^5)^7$, **multiply** the indices, that is,
$$(a^5)^7 = a^{5 \times 7} = a^{35}$$

Examples: $(x^5)^2 = x^5 \times x^5 = x^{10}$

$(3m^4)^3 = 27m^{12}$

Index laws

Examples:

1. $a^m \times a^n = a^{m+n}$ $2^5 \times 2^3 = 2^8 = 256$

2. $\dfrac{a^m}{a^n} = a^{m-n}$ $2^5 \div 2^3 = 2^2 = 4$

3. $(a^m)^n = a^{mn}$ $(2^5)^3 = 2^{15} = 32768$

4. $a^m \times b^m = (ab)^m$ $2^5 \times 3^5 = 6^5 = 7776$

5. $a^0 = 1$ (if $a \neq 0$) $2^0 = 1$

6. $a^{-m} = \dfrac{1}{a^m}$ $2^{-5} = \dfrac{1}{2^5} = \dfrac{1}{32}$

7. $a^{\frac{1}{q}} = \sqrt[q]{a}$ $8^{\frac{1}{3}} = \sqrt[3]{8} = 2$

8. $a^{\frac{p}{q}} = \left(\sqrt[q]{a}\right)^p = \sqrt[q]{a^p}$ $16^{\frac{3}{4}} = \left(\sqrt[4]{16}\right)^3 = 2^3 = 8$

Solving equations

One-step   Examples: $x + 5 = 13 \Rightarrow x = 8$

$x - 5 = 13 \Rightarrow x = 18$

$3x = 15 \Rightarrow x = 5$

$\dfrac{x}{5} = 3 \Rightarrow x = 15$

Two-step   Example: $2x + 5 = 23$

$2x = 18$

$x = 9$

Three-step
Examples:

$$\frac{2x+5}{7} = 3 \qquad 3(4y+1) = 39$$
$$2x+5 = 21 \qquad 12y+3 = 39$$
$$2x = 16 \qquad 12y = 36$$
$$x = 8 \qquad y = 3$$

Solving simple problems using equations

A number is 7 more than a second number. Their sum is 25. What are the numbers?

Let the first number be n. The second number must be $n-7$.

$$\text{So } n+n-7 = 25$$
$$2n-7 = 25$$
$$2n = 32$$
$$n = 16$$

Therefore the numbers are 16 and 9.

Solving more complex equations

$$\frac{x-5}{3} - \frac{2x+1}{4} = 7$$
$$4(x-5) - 3(2x+1) = 84 \quad \text{(multiplying both sides by the LCD, 12)}$$
$$4x - 20 - 6x - 3 = 84$$
$$-2x - 23 = 84$$
$$-2x = 107$$
$$x = \frac{107}{-2}$$
$$x = -53\frac{1}{2}$$

Simple inequations, graphing solutions on the number line

$$3x + 7 < 40$$
$$3x < 33$$
$$x < 11$$

```
  |———————←———○———|———————|
  9      10     11     12     13
```

$$6 < 2x - 5 \leq 13$$
$$11 < 2x \leq 18$$
$$5\tfrac{1}{2} < x \leq 9$$

```
——|————|——○————————●——|——
  4    5   6   7   8   9   10
```

The open circle *excludes* the x-value $5\tfrac{1}{2}$, and the filled-in circle *includes* the x-value 9.

Formulas

A **formula** is an equation in terms of pronumerals to represent a relationship between two or more quantities.

For example, $A = lb$ represents the relationship between area, length and width of a rectangle. A is the *subject* of the formula.

So if $l = 23$ cm and $b = 11$ cm, then $A = 23 \times 11 = 253$ cm².

Construction of formulas

Example:

Consider a square garden of side g m. A concrete path of width c surrounds a square lawn of side l as illustrated

Write down a formula for:

(a) c in terms of g and l;
(b) the area of the path in terms of g and l.

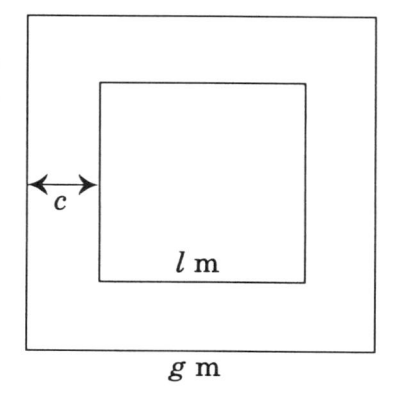

(a) The difference between the width of the garden and the width of the lawn is equal to twice the width of the path.
$$g = l + 2c$$
$$2c = g - l$$
$$c = \frac{g - l}{2}$$

(b) The area of the square garden is $g \times g$, the area of the square lawn is $l \times l$. The area of the path is the difference of the two:
$$\text{Area} = g^2 - l^2 \text{ m}^2$$

Changing the subject

Example: Change the subject of $v = u + at$ to t.

$$u + at = v$$
$$at = v - u$$
$$t = \frac{v - u}{a}$$

Simultaneous equations

By elimination

Example: Solve simultaneously the equations:
$$3x + 5y = 7$$
$$2x - 3y = 11$$

Solution:

	$3x + 5y = 7$	...(1)
	$2x - 3y = 11$	...(2)
$(1) \times 3$	$9x + 15y = 21$	...(1a)
$(2) \times 5$	$10x - 15y = 55$	...(2a)
$(1a) + (2a):$	$19x = 76$	
	$x = 4$	

Sub. into (1): $12 + 5y = 7$
$$5y = -5$$
$$y = -1$$

$\therefore x = 4, y = -1$.

By substitution

Example: Solve simultaneously the equations:
$$y = 12 - 2x$$
$$5x - 3y = 19$$

Solution:
$$y = 12 - 2x \quad ...(1)$$
$$5x - 3y = 19 \quad ...(2)$$

Sub. (1) into (2): $5x - 3(12 - 2x) = 19$
$$5x - 36 + 6x = 19$$
$$11x = 55$$
$$x = 5$$

Sub. into (1): $y = 12 - 2 \times 5$
$$y = 2$$

$\therefore x = 5, y = 2$.

Quadratic equations

By factorisation

Example: Solve for x: $x^2 - 7x + 10 = 0$

Solution:
$$x^2 - 7x + 10 = 0$$
$$(x-2)(x-5) = 0$$
$$x - 2 = 0 \text{ or } x - 5 = 0$$
$$\therefore x = 2, 5.$$

By completing the square

Example: Solve for x: $x^2 + 8x + 5 = 0$

Solution:
$$x^2 + 8x + 5 = 0$$
$$x^2 + 8x = -5$$

Halve the coefficient of x, square it, and add the square to both sides.
$$x^2 + 8x + 16 = 11$$
$$(x+4)^2 = 11$$
$$x + 4 = \pm\sqrt{11}$$
$$x = -4 \pm \sqrt{11}$$

By the quadratic formula

Example: Solve for x: $3x^2 - 11x + 7 = 0$

Solution: To solve a quadratic equation of the form $ax^2 + bx + c = 0$, use the formula:

$$\boxed{x = \frac{-b \pm \sqrt{b^2 - 4ac}}{2a}}$$

$$x = \frac{-(-11) \pm \sqrt{(-11)^2 - 4(3)(7)}}{2(3)}$$

$$x = \frac{11 \pm \sqrt{37}}{6}$$

Chapter 3
GEOMETRY

Geometry is a branch of mathematics which involves the study of properties of points, lines, planes, and of curves, shapes and solids.

Plane shapes

A **polygon** is a many-sided closed figure. For example, a pentagon is a five-sided figure.

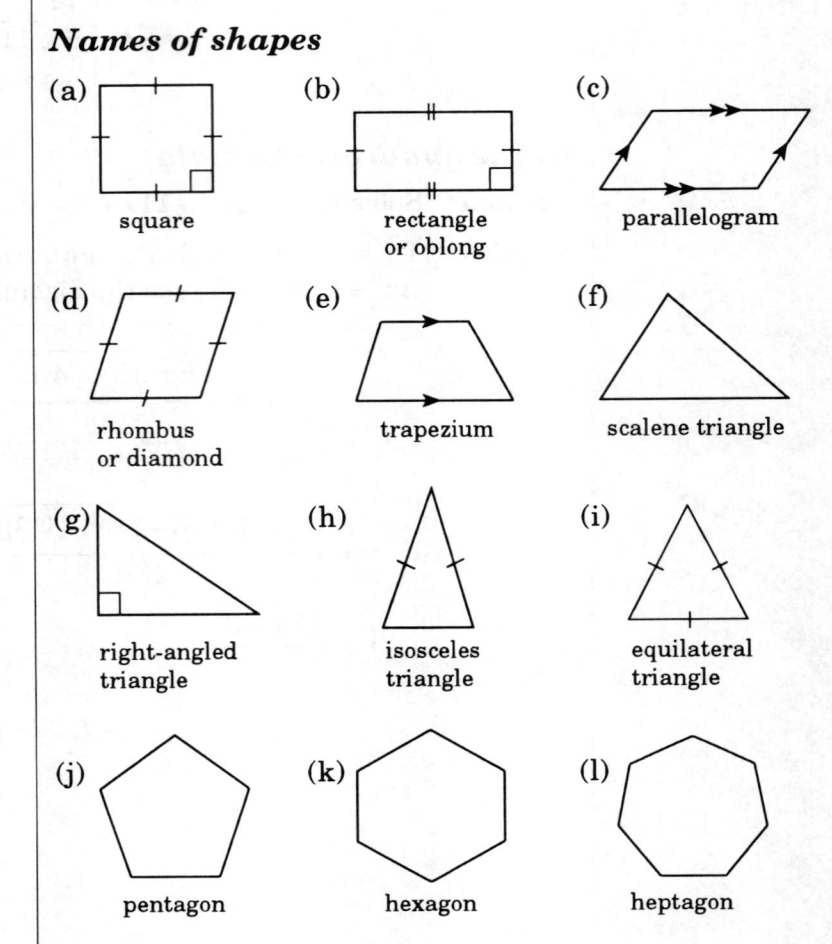

Names of shapes

(a) square

(b) rectangle or oblong

(c) parallelogram

(d) rhombus or diamond

(e) trapezium

(f) scalene triangle

(g) right-angled triangle

(h) isosceles triangle

(i) equilateral triangle

(j) pentagon

(k) hexagon

(l) heptagon

(m) octagon (n) nonagon (o) decagon

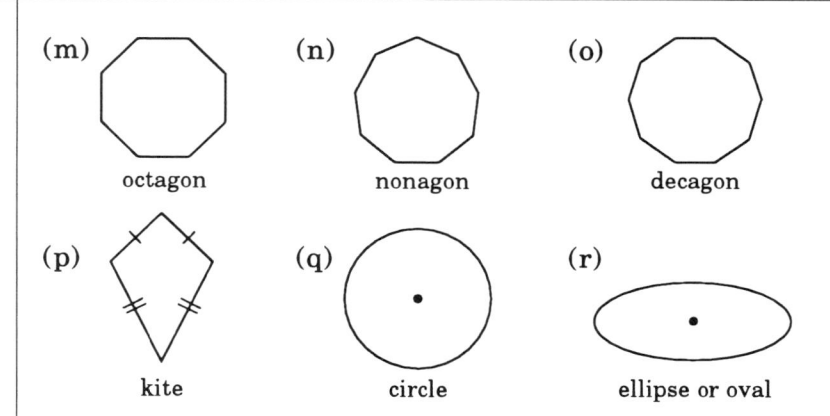

(p) kite (q) circle (r) ellipse or oval

Transformations

Any shape can be moved to a new position, without changing its shape, by sliding it, spinning it, or flipping it.

- A slide is called a **translation**.

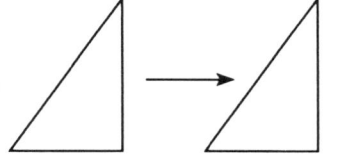

- A spin is called a **rotation**.

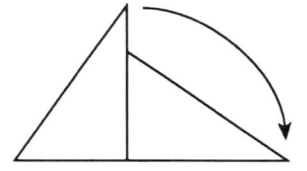

- A flip is called a **reflection**.

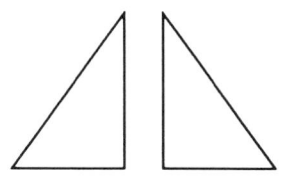

Symmetry

- A shape has **line symmetry** if it can be divided by a line into two identical halves which are mirror images of each other. The dividing line is called the **axis of symmetry**.

If a shape has two axes of symmetry then it is said to have line symmetry of **order 2**. If it has three axes then it is of order 3, etc.

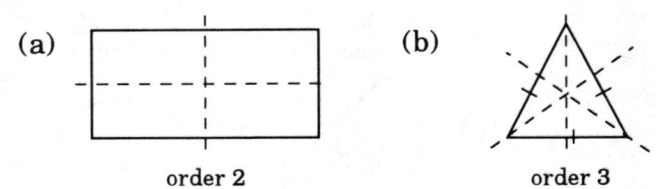

(a) order 2

(b) order 3

❑ A shape has **rotational symmetry** if it can be spun about a point so that it repeats its shape more than once during one rotation. The point about which the shape spins is called the **centre of symmetry**.

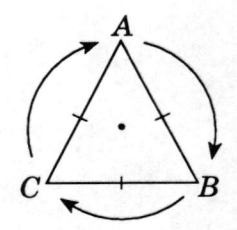

If the shape is repeated two times in one revolution then it is said to have rotational symmetry of **order 2**. If it is repeated three times then the order is 3, etc.

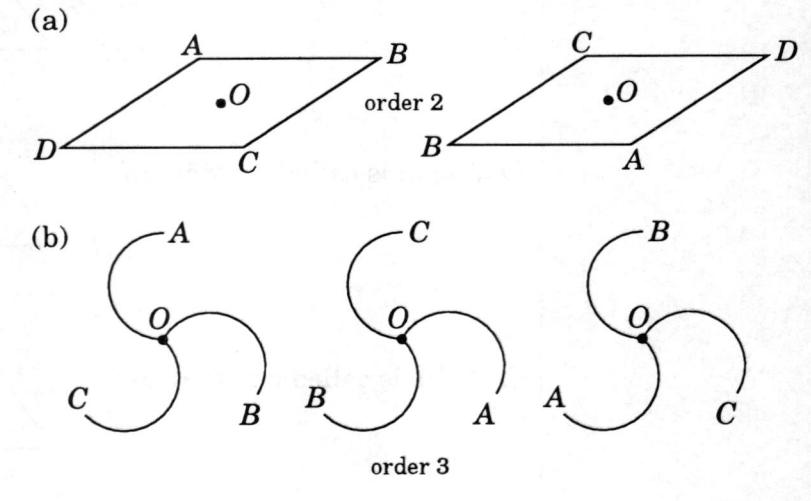

(a) order 2

(b) order 3

❑ If a shape repeats itself after a half-turn (that is, 180°), then it is said to have **point symmetry**. Thus all rotational symmetries of **even** order have point symmetry.

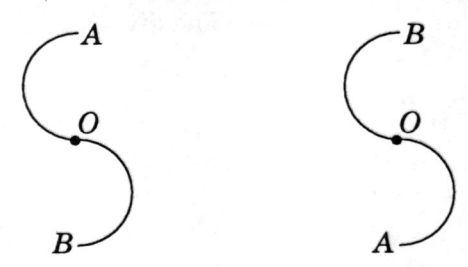

Parts of a circle

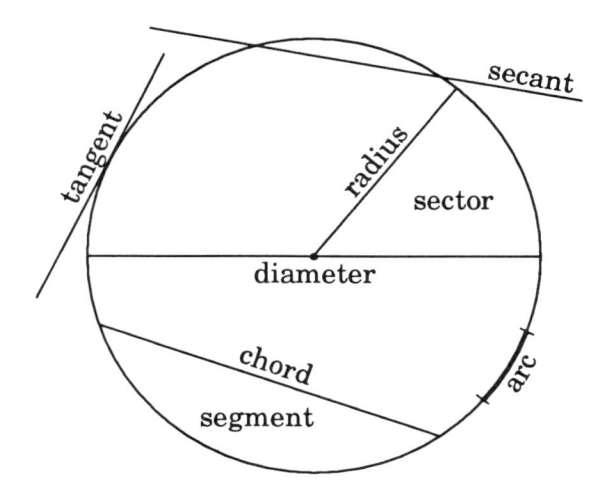

Labels on circle diagram: secant, tangent, radius, sector, diameter, chord, arc, segment

Solid shapes

Names of solids

Solid shapes have three dimensions: length, breadth, and depth.

There are two main types of solids with plane-shaped faces:
prisms and **pyramids**

Solid shapes have various parts:

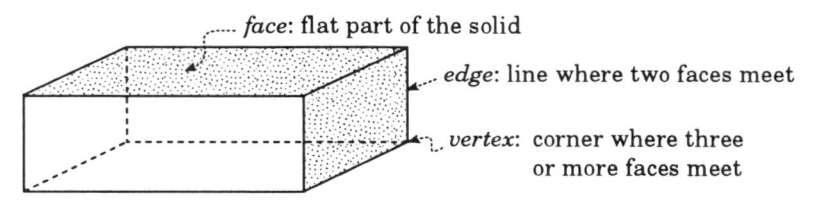

face: flat part of the solid
edge: line where two faces meet
vertex: corner where three or more faces meet

❑ **Prisms** have a special pair of parallel faces, called a **cross-section**. These faces are the only ones that need not be rectangular. A prism is named according to its cross-section.

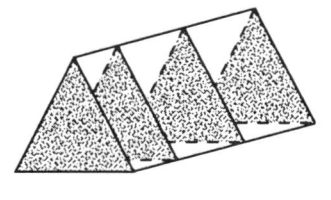

triangular prism

❏ **Pyramids** have polygons for the base, with the other faces being triangles meeting at a common *vertex*.

A pyramid is named according to the shape of its base.

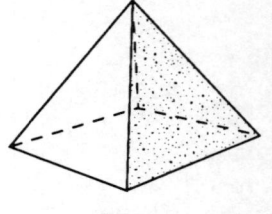

square pyramid

Some solids are **neither** prisms, **nor** pyramids.
The most common are the *cylinder*, the *cone*, and the *sphere*.

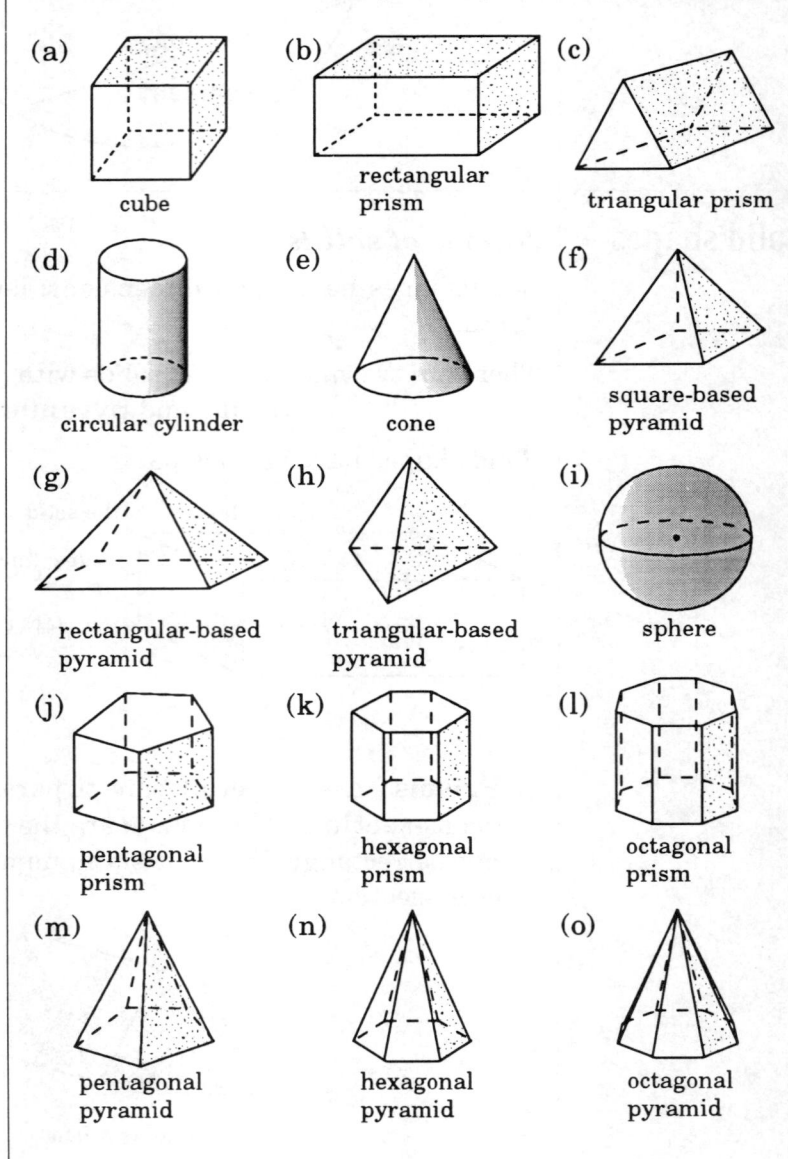

(a) cube

(b) rectangular prism

(c) triangular prism

(d) circular cylinder

(e) cone

(f) square-based pyramid

(g) rectangular-based pyramid

(h) triangular-based pyramid

(i) sphere

(j) pentagonal prism

(k) hexagonal prism

(l) octagonal prism

(m) pentagonal pyramid

(n) hexagonal pyramid

(o) octagonal pyramid

Nets

Solid shapes can be made up of plane shapes. The plane shapes are folded along common edges to form the solid.

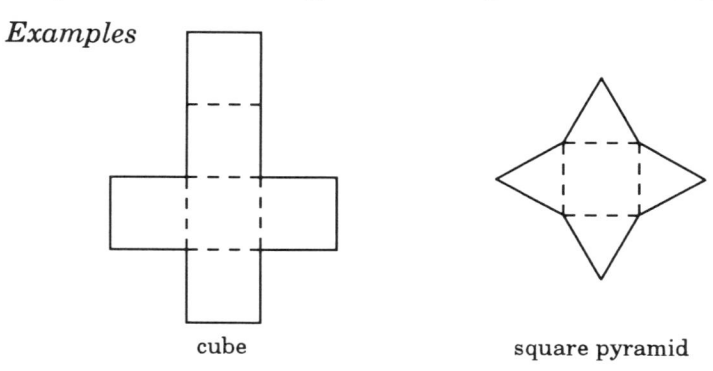

Examples

cube

square pyramid

Angles

An **angle** is the measure of turning between two rays about a common end-point.

Naming angles

There are several different ways of naming angles.

$\angle ABC$ or $\angle CBA$ or $A\hat{B}C$ or $C\hat{B}A$ or $\angle B$ or $\hat{B}$

Types of angles

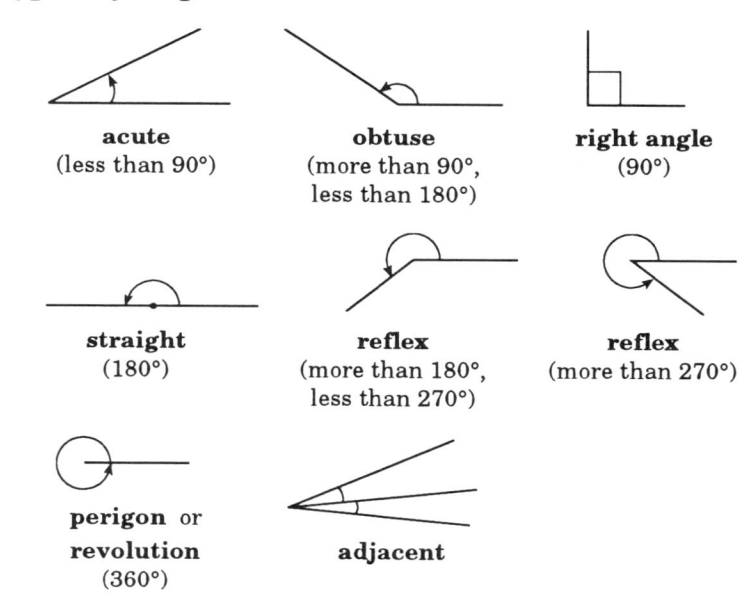

acute
(less than 90°)

obtuse
(more than 90°, less than 180°)

right angle
(90°)

straight
(180°)

reflex
(more than 180°, less than 270°)

reflex
(more than 270°)

perigon or **revolution**
(360°)

adjacent

- **Adjacent** angles share a common arm **and** a common vertex.

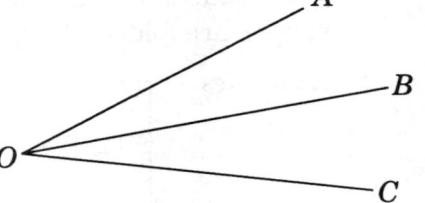

$\angle AOB$ and $\angle BOC$ are adjacent angles.

- **Complementary angles** add up to **90°**.

$\angle ABD + \angle DBC = 90°$

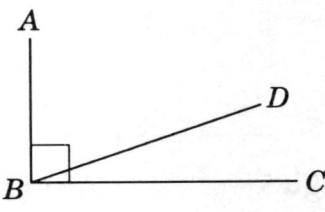

- **Supplementary angles** add up to **180°**.

$\angle AOC + \angle COB = 180°$

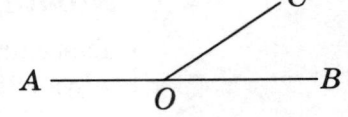

Measuring angles

Place the centre of the protractor on the vertex of the angle and set 0° on one arm of the angle. Then read the measurement on the protractor coinciding with the other arm.

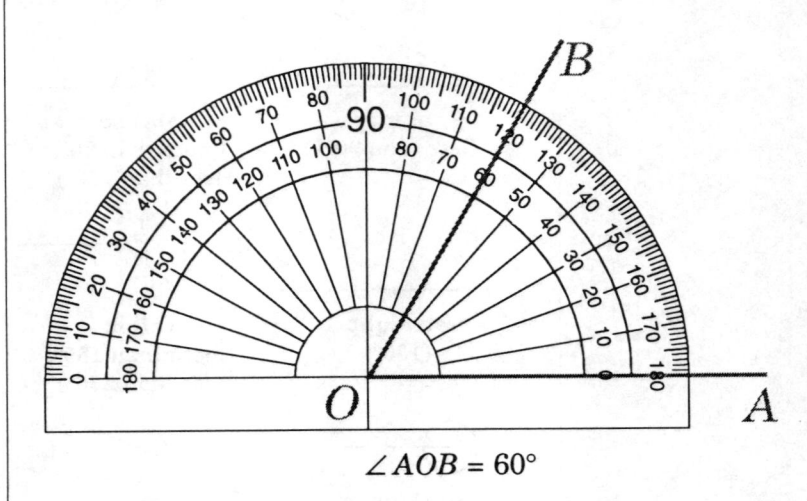

$\angle AOB = 60°$

Angles related to two lines cut by a transversal

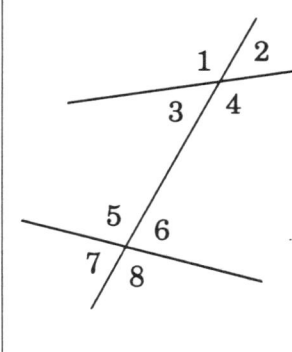

1 and 5 are a pair of **corresponding** angles
2 and 6 are a pair of **corresponding** angles
3 and 7 are a pair of **corresponding** angles
4 and 8 are a pair of **corresponding** angles
3 and 6 are a pair of **alternate** angles
4 and 5 are a pair of **alternate** angles
3 and 5 are a pair of **cointerior** angles
4 and 6 are a pair of **cointerior** angles

Pythagoras' theorem

Hypotenuse

The longest side of a right-angled triangle is called the **hypotenuse**. The hypotenuse is opposite the right angle.

Definition

In any right-angled triangle, the square on the hypotenuse is equal to the sum of the squares on the other two sides.

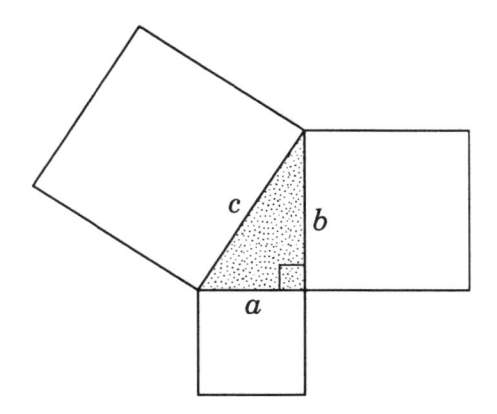

$$c^2 = a^2 + b^2$$

Application

Find h.

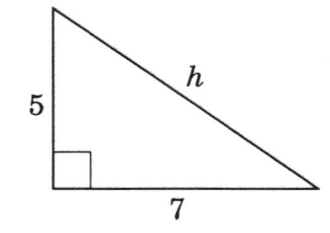

$$h^2 = 5^2 + 7^2$$
$$= 25 + 49$$
$$= 74$$
$$h = \sqrt{74}$$

Find x.

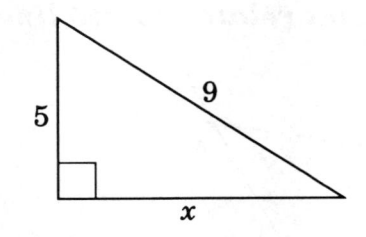

$$9^2 = 5^2 + x^2$$
$$x^2 = 81 - 25$$
$$= 56$$
$$x = \sqrt{56}$$

Reasoning and theorems

Symbols

≡	is congruent to
⫴	is similar to
⊥	is perpendicular to
∥	is parallel to
∠	angle
△	triangle
∴	therefore
∵	because
parm or ∥gram	parallelogram

Angles at a point

The sum of all the angles at a point is 360°.

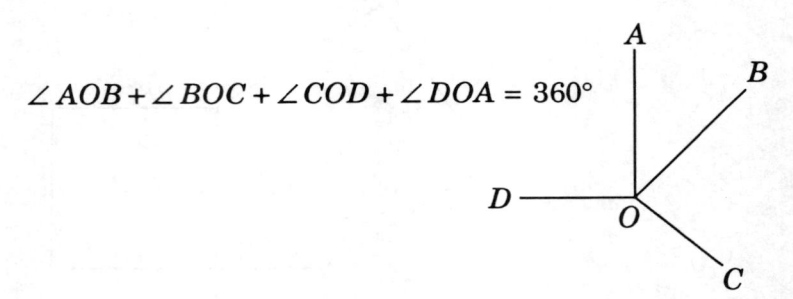

$$\angle AOB + \angle BOC + \angle COD + \angle DOA = 360°$$

Vertically opposite angles

When two lines intersect, each pair of vertically opposite angles is equal.

$$\angle AXC = \angle BXD$$
$$\angle AXD = \angle BXC$$

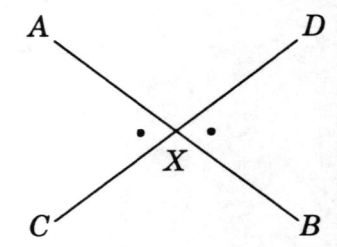

Angles of parallel lines

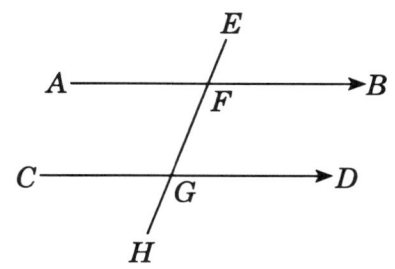

two parallel lines cut by a *transversal*

When two parallel lines are cut by a transversal, then:

❏ each pair of corresponding angles is equal:

- ∠AFE = ∠CGF
- ∠BFE = ∠DGF
- ∠AFG = ∠CGH
- ∠BFG = ∠DGH

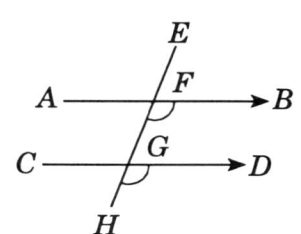

❏ each pair of alternate angles is equal:

- ∠AFG = ∠DGF
- ∠BFG = ∠CGF

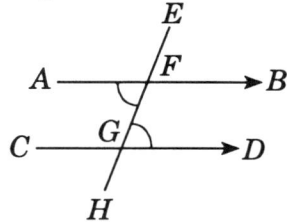

❏ each pair of cointerior angles is supplementary:

- ∠AFG + ∠CGF = 180°
- ∠BFG + ∠DGF = 180°

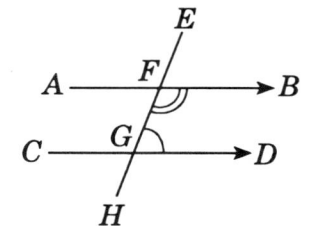

Angle sum of triangle

The sum of the three interior angles of a triangle is 180°.

∠A + ∠B + ∠C = 180°

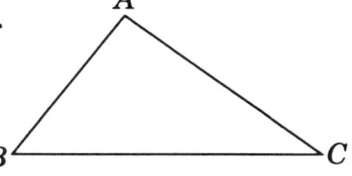

Angle sum of quadrilateral

The sum of the four interior angles of a quadrilateral is 360°.

$\angle A + \angle B + \angle C + \angle D = 360°$

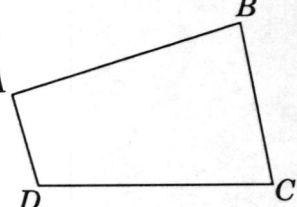

Isosceles triangles

An isosceles triangle has two equal sides.

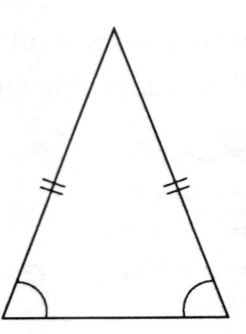

The base angles (opposite the equal sides) of an isosceles triangle are equal.

Equilateral triangles

Equilateral triangles have three equal sides, and three equal angles, each measuring 60°.

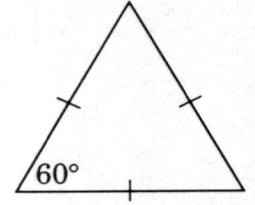

Exterior angle of a triangle

If a side of a triangle is produced beyond the vertex, an exterior angle is formed.

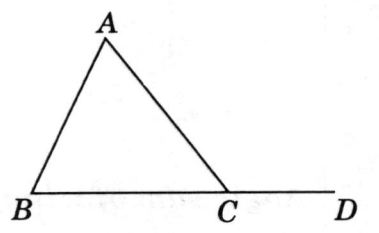

The exterior angle of a triangle is equal to the sum of the two interior opposite angles.

$$\angle ACD = \angle ABC + \angle BAC$$

Numerical problems

1 $AB \parallel CD$ Find $\angle CGH$, giving reasons.

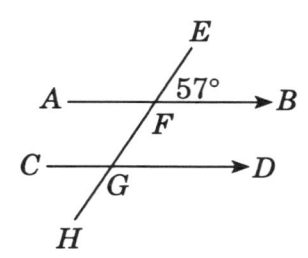

$\angle AFG = 57°$ (vertically opposite to $\angle EFB$)
$\angle CGH = 57°$ (corresponding $\angle$s of $\parallel$ lines, $AB \parallel CD$)

2 $PQ = PR$. Find x.

Since $PQ = PR$, $\triangle PQR$ is isosceles,

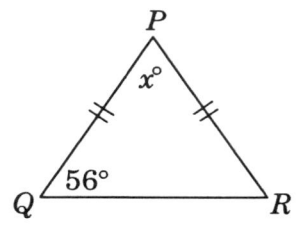

$\therefore \quad \angle PRQ = \angle PQR$ (base $\angle$s of isosc. $\triangle$ are =)
$\therefore \quad \angle PRQ = 56°$ (since $\angle PQR = 56°$, given)
$\quad\quad x + 112° = 180°$ ($\angle$ sum of $\triangle$)
$\therefore \quad\quad x = 68°$

Constructions with ruler and compass

Bisecting intervals

With radius greater than half the interval, arcs are drawn from each end to intersect above and below the interval. These points of intersection are joined, to bisect the interval.

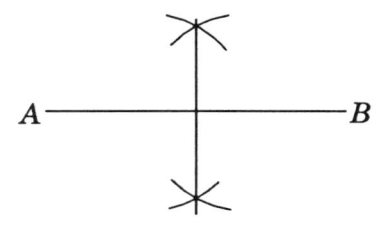

Bisecting angles

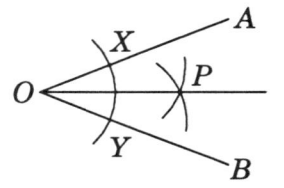

With centre O, draw arc XY. Then draw two more arcs from X and Y to intersect at P. Join OP.

Copying angles

Draw OP. Draw arc CD from E, and with the same radius draw arc QR from O.

Then with radius CD draw an arc from Q to meet arc QR. Join OR.

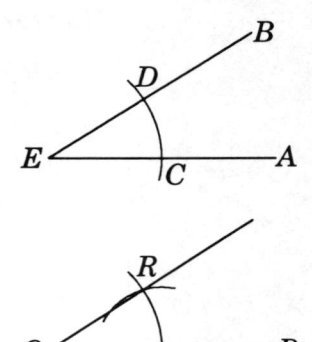

Constructing an angle of 60°

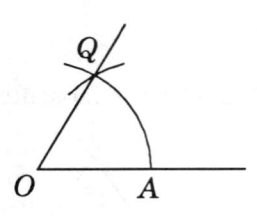

With O as centre, draw an arc of radius OA. With the same radius, draw an arc from A to meet this arc at Q. Join OQ.

To construct an angle of 30° bisect a 60° angle.

Constructing an angle of 90°

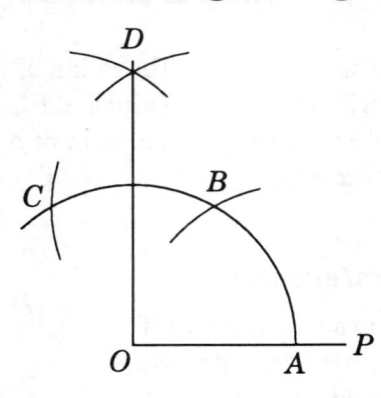

With centre O, draw an arc of radius OA. With the same radius, draw an arc from A to cut the first arc at B, and from B draw another arc to cut the first arc at C. With B and C as centres, draw arcs to meet at D. Join OD.

Constructing parallel lines

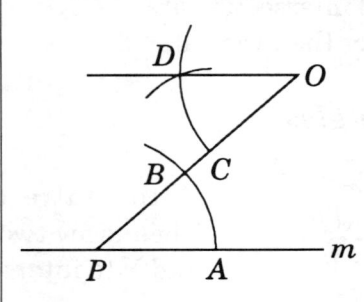

Draw a line from O to meet line m at P. With centre P, draw arc AB. With the same radius and centre O, draw an arc from C. With centre C, draw arc at D with radius AB. Join OD.

Constructing perpendicular lines

❑ From an internal point:

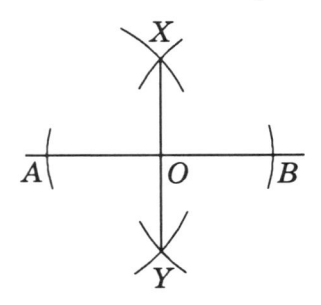

With O as centre, mark off arcs at A and B such that $OA = OB$. With radius greater than OA, draw arcs from A and B to intersect at X and Y. Join XY.

❑ From an external point:

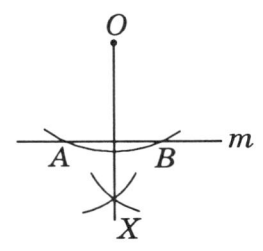

From the external point O, draw an arc to meet line m at A and B. With centres A and B, draw arcs with radius more than $\frac{1}{2}AB$ to meet at X. Join OX.

Congruent triangles

Two triangles are **congruent** if they are equal in every respect, that is, they are the same size and shape.

Theorems

Two triangles are congruent if and only if:

❑ three sides of one are respectively equal to three sides of the other **(SSS)**

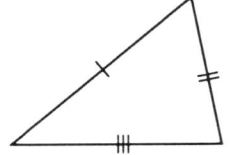

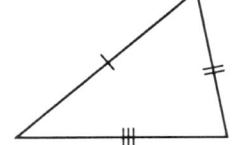

(a) (b)

❑ two sides and the included angle of one are respectively equal to two sides and the included angle of the other **(SAS)**

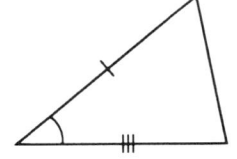

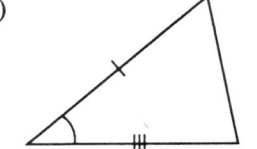

(a) (b)

❏ two angles and a side of one are respectively equal to two angles and the corresponding side of the other   **(AAS)**

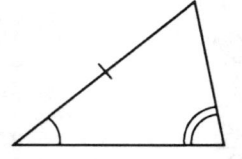

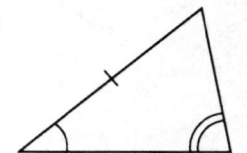

(a)   (b)

❏ the hypotenuse and a side of a right-triangle are respectively equal to the hypotenuse and a side of the other right-triangle   **(RHS)**

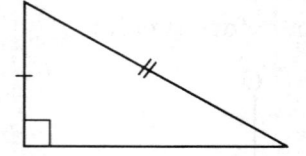

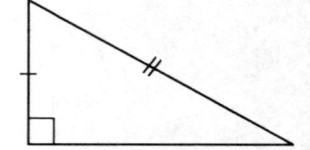

(a)   (b)

Proofs and application

ABC is an isosceles triangle in which $AB = AC$. P and Q are points on BC such that $BP = CQ$.

Prove that APQ is isosceles.

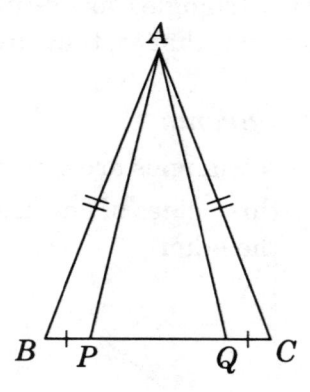

In $\triangle$s ABP and ACQ,

$\quad\quad AB = AC \quad\quad$ (given)
$\quad\quad BP = CQ \quad\quad$ (given)
$\quad\quad \angle ABP = \angle ACQ \quad$ (base $\angle$s of isosc. $\triangle$)
$\therefore \quad \triangle ABP \equiv \triangle ACQ \quad$ (**SAS**)
$\therefore \quad\quad AP = AQ \quad\quad$ (corresp. sides of congr. $\triangle$s)
$\therefore \quad \triangle APQ$ is isosceles (since 2 sides are equal)

Similarity

Two triangles are **similar** if they are the same shape.

Theorems

Two triangles are similar if and only if:

- two angles of one are respectively equal to two angles of the other, that is, $\angle A = \angle D$ and $\angle B = \angle E$ or
$\angle A = \angle D$ and $\angle C = \angle F$ or
i.e. $\angle B = \angle E$ and $\angle C = \angle F$

(a) A, B, C

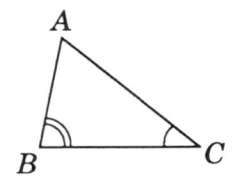

(b) D, E, F

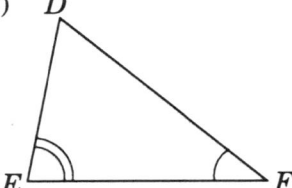

- the lengths of corresponding sides are in proportion, that is, $\dfrac{a}{d} = \dfrac{b}{e} = \dfrac{c}{f}$

(a)

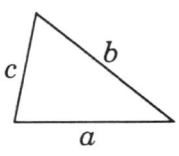

(b)

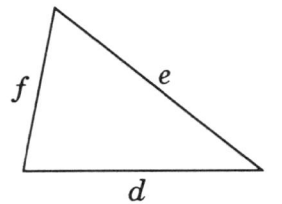

- an angle of one is equal to an angle of the other and the sides about these angles are in proportion

(a) A, B, C

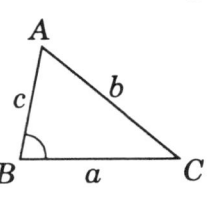

(b) D, E, F

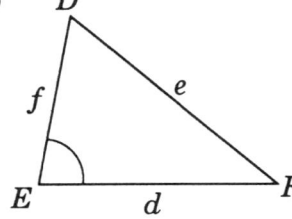

$\angle A = \angle D$ and $\dfrac{b}{e} = \dfrac{c}{f}$ or

$\angle B = \angle E$ and $\dfrac{c}{f} = \dfrac{a}{d}$ or

$\angle C = \angle F$ and $\dfrac{a}{d} = \dfrac{b}{e}$

The areas of similar triangles are in the ratio of the squares of corresponding sides.

$$\frac{\triangle ABC}{\triangle DEF} = \frac{a^2}{d^2} = \frac{b^2}{e^2} = \frac{c^2}{f^2}$$

Calculation of sides

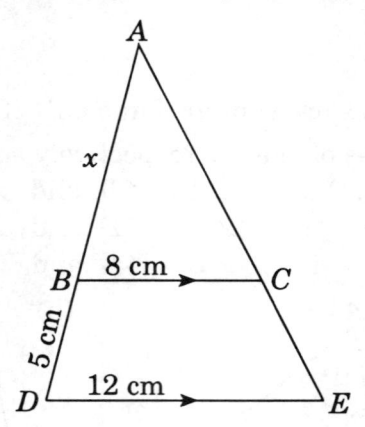

$\triangle ABC \; ||| \; \triangle ADE$ Find AB.

Let $AB = x$

$$\frac{x}{x+5} = \frac{8}{12}$$

$$\frac{x}{x+5} = \frac{2}{3}$$

$$3x = 2x + 10$$

$$x = 10$$

$\therefore \qquad AB = 10 \text{ cm}$

Properties of quadrilaterals

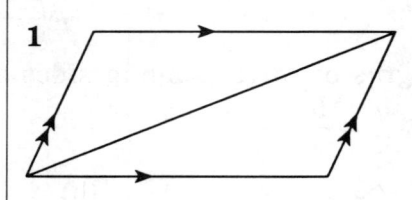

1 Any diagonal forms two congruent triangles with the sides of a parallelogram.

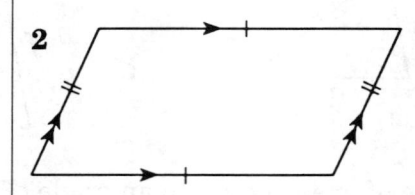

2 The opposite sides of a parallelogram are equal and parallel.

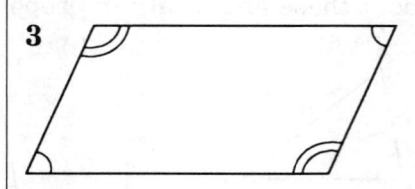

3 The opposite angles of a parallelogram are equal.

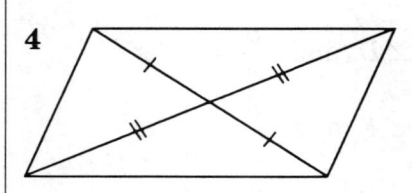

4 The diagonals of any parallelogram bisect each other.

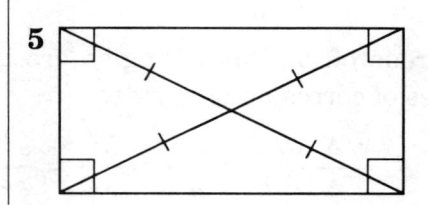

5 In any rectangle all the angles are right angles and the diagonals are equal and bisect each other.

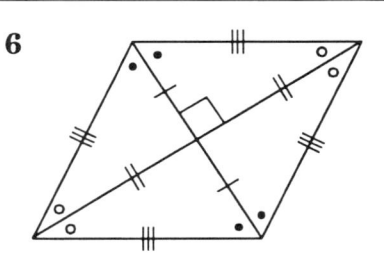

6. A rhombus has all its sides equal. The diagonals bisect each other at right angles and bisect the angles of the rhombus.

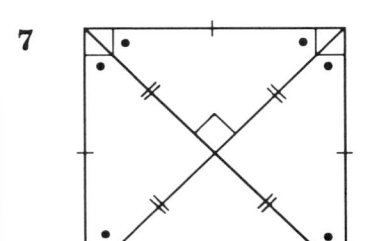

7. A square has all its sides equal, and all its angles right angles. The diagonals are equal, bisect each other at right angles and bisect the angles of the square.

Geometry of the circle

Circle properties

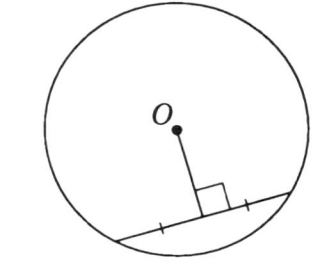

1. A line through the centre of a circle perpendicular to a chord bisects that chord.

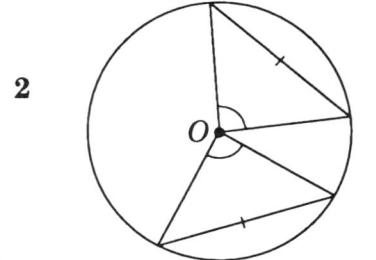

2. Equal chords of a circle subtend equal angles at the centre.

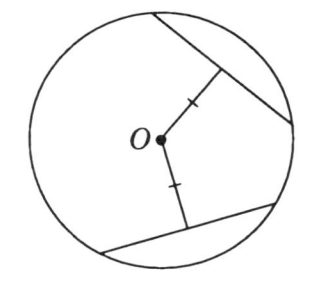

3. Equal chords of a circle are equidistant from the centre.

Angle theorems of the circle

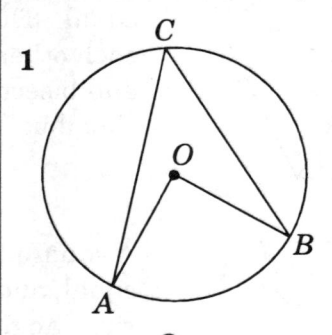

1 An angle at the centre of a circle is double the size of an angle at the circumference when standing on the same arc, that is,

$$\angle AOB = 2 \times \angle ACB.$$

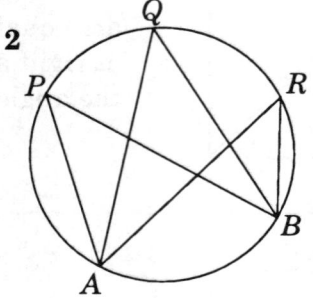

2 Angles in the same segment of a circle are equal, that is,

$$\angle APB = \angle AQB = \angle ARB = \text{etc.}$$

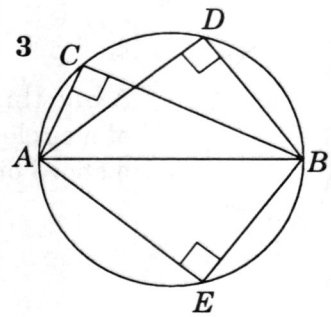

3 Any angle in a semicircle is a right angle, that is,

$$\angle ACB = \angle ADB = \angle AEB = 90°$$

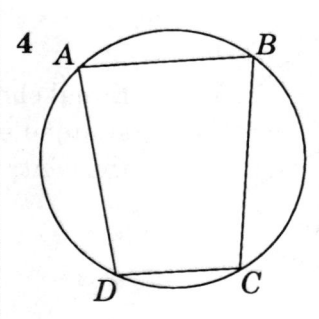

4 A cyclic quadrilateral has all four vertices on the circumference of a circle. Opposite angles of a cyclic quadrilateral are supplementary, that is,

$$\angle A + \angle C = 180° \text{ and}$$
$$\angle B + \angle D = 180°.$$

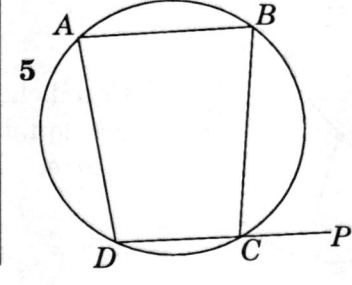

5 The exterior angle of a cyclic quadrilateral is equal to the interior opposite angle, that is,

$$\angle BCP = \angle A.$$

Tangent theorems of the circle

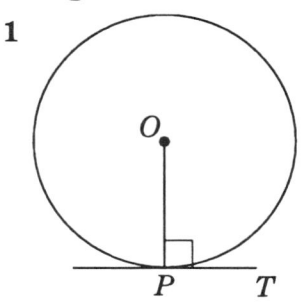

1 A line through a given point on a circle is a tangent to the circle if and only if it is perpendicular to the radius at the point of contact, that is, $\angle OPT = 90°$

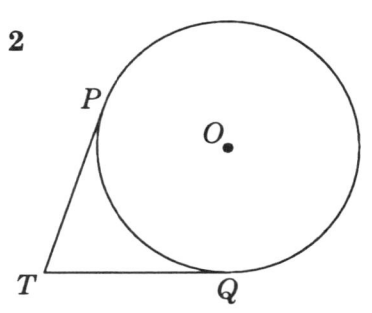

2 The tangents to a circle from a given external point are equal in length, that is, $PT = QT$.

Chord theorems of the circle

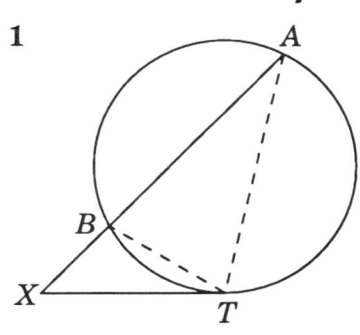

1 If any chord of a circle is divided externally at a point, then the product of the segments is equal to the square of the tangent to the circle from this point, that is,

$$XT^2 = XA \cdot XB$$

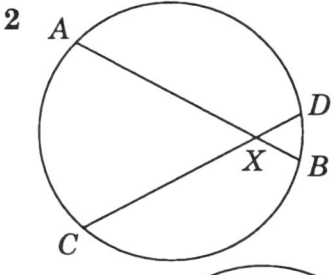

2 If two chords of a circle intersect internally or externally, then the point of intersection divides the chord into line segments such that the products of the segments on both chords are equal, that is,

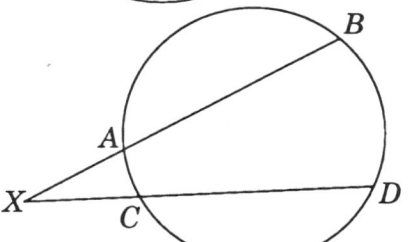

$$AX \cdot XB = CX \cdot XD$$

Alternate segment theorem

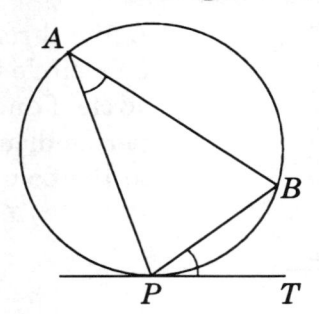

An angle formed by a tangent to a circle and a chord drawn to the point of contact is equal to any angle in the alternate segment, that is, $\angle BPT = \angle BAP$.

Further reasoning

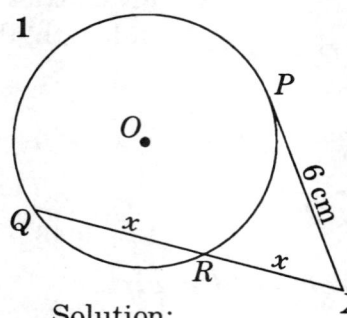

1 PX is a tangent of length 6 cm to a circle with centre O. Q is a point on the circle and QX cuts the circle again at R such that $QR = RX$.

Find the length of the chord QR.

Solution:
Let $QR = x$ cm $= RX$.

Then $XP^2 = XQ \cdot XR$ (sq. on tangt. = prod. of segmts.)

$\therefore \qquad 6^2 = x \cdot 2x$

$\qquad 2x^2 = 36$

$\qquad x^2 = 18$

$\qquad x = \sqrt{18}$

$\qquad x = 3\sqrt{2}$

$\therefore QR$ is $3\sqrt{2}$ cm.

2 RT is a tangent to a circle. P, Q and R are on the circle such that $PR = QR$.

Prove that $PQ \parallel RT$.

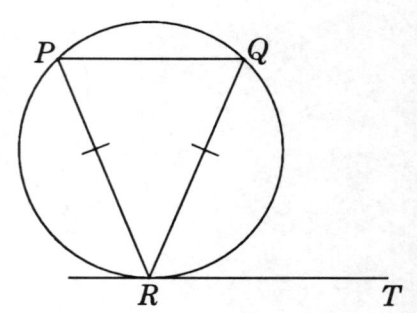

Solution:

$\quad \angle QRT = \angle QPR$ (alt. segment theorem)
$\quad \angle QPR = \angle PQR$ (base $\angle$s of isos. $\triangle$)
$\therefore \angle QRT = \angle PQR$ (equal to same $\angle$)
$\therefore PQ \parallel RT$ (since alt. $\angle$s are =)

Chapter 4
MEASUREMENT

Units and symbols

In the metric system the basic unit of:
- **length** is the **metre**, symbol **m**,
- **mass** is the **gram**, symbol **g**,
- **capacity** is the **litre**, symbol **L**.

(In SI units the standard unit of mass is the kilogram.)

A prefix is placed before each unit for a multiple of that unit.

Prefix	Symbol	Meaning	Value
Mega	M	million	1 000 000
kilo	k	thousand	1000
hecto	h	hundred	100
deca	da	ten	10
deci	d	tenth	$\frac{1}{10}$
centi	c	hundredth	$\frac{1}{100}$
milli	m	thousandth	$\frac{1}{1000}$
micro	μ	millionth	$\frac{1}{1\,000\,000}$

The most commonly used prefixes are **kilo**, **centi**, and **milli**.

So,

1 kilometre	=	1000 metres
	=	100 000 centimetres
	=	1 000 000 millimetres
1 metre	=	100 centimetres
	=	1000 millimetres
1 centimetre	=	10 millimetres

Examples:

$$2.54 \text{ m} = 2.54 \times 100$$
$$= 254 \text{ cm}$$

$$458 \text{ cm} = 458 \div 100$$
$$= 4.58 \text{ m}$$

To convert small units into large units we **divide** by the required power of 10.

To convert large units into small units we **multiply** by the required power of 10.

Time and calendar

- 1 year is the time taken by the earth to orbit the sun
- 1 day is the time for the earth to rotate once on its axis
- 1 year = 365 days, 1 leap year = 366 days
- 1 year = 52 weeks, 1 year = 12 months
- 1 day = 24 hours
- 1 hour = 60 minutes
- 1 minute = 60 seconds
- a.m. – between 12 midnight and 12 noon
- p.m. – between 12 noon and 12 midnight

Measuring instruments

- A **ruler** is used as a straight edge to draw straight lines as well as to measure the length of a line.

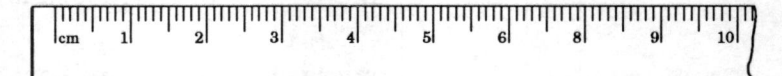

❏ There are two types of **set squares**, a 60–30 set square and a 45 set square.

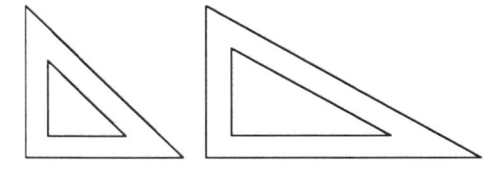

Set squares can be used in conjunction with a ruler to draw perpendicular as well as parallel lines.

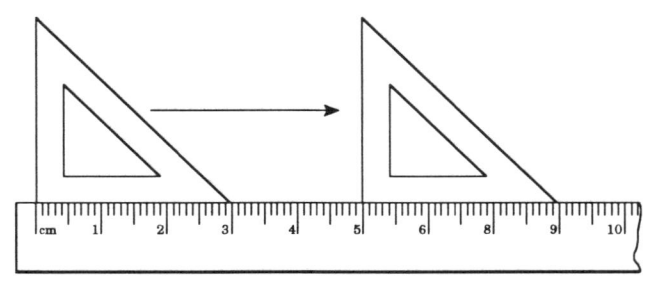

❏ A **compass** is used to draw circles or arcs of circles. It consists of two rigid arms joined by a hinge. At one end is a sharp point which is placed at the centre of the circle. At the other end there is a pencil or marker which traces out the circumference of the circle or the arc.

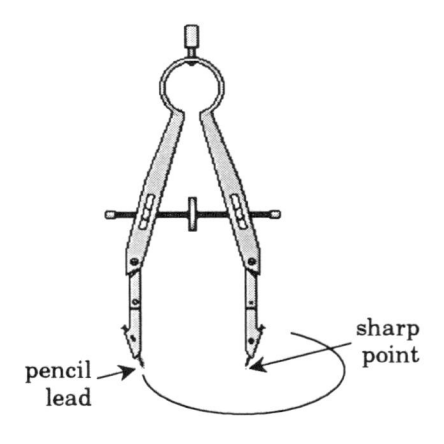

❏ A **protractor** is used to measure or mark out angles. There are two scales so we can measure angles both clockwise and anticlockwise.

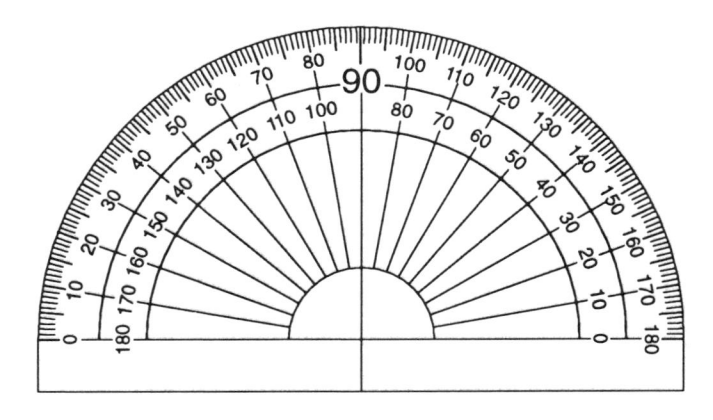

Mensuration

This is the measuring of geometrical quantities such as lengths, areas, and volumes.

Perimeter

The **perimeter** of a shape is the distance around the shape, that is, the length of the boundary. It is found by adding up the lengths of the sides of the figure.

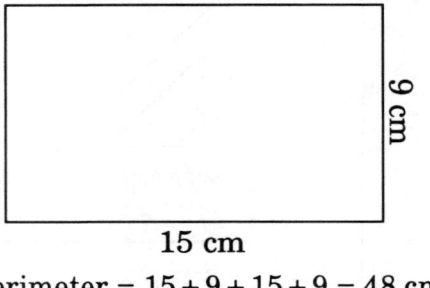

perimeter = 15 + 9 + 15 + 9 = 48 cm

Area

The **area** of a shape is the measure of the size of its surface. It is measured in square units.

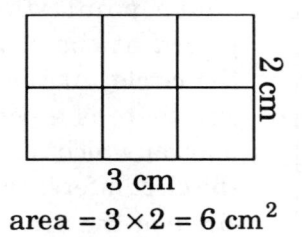

area = 3 × 2 = 6 cm^2

Volume

The **volume** of a solid is the measure of the amount of space occupied by the solid. It is measured in cubic units.

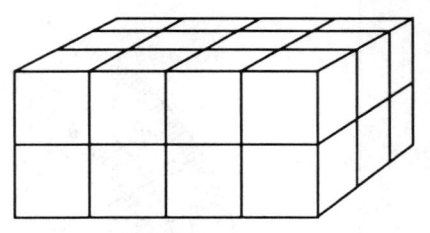

volume = 4 × 3 × 2 = 24 cm^3

The volume of all prisms and cylinders is found by multiplying the cross-sectional area by the perpendicular height of the prism or cylinder.

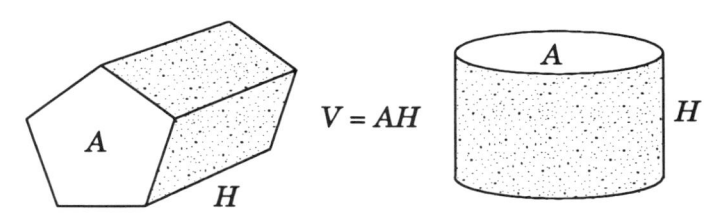

$V = AH$

The volume of all pyramids and cones is equal to $\frac{1}{3}$ of the volume of the equivalent prism or cylinder.

Capacity

Capacity is the ability to hold a certain volume. It is measured in units such as litres, millilitres, etc.

Mass

Mass is the bulk of a solid body. It is measured in units such as grams, kilograms, etc.

Surface area (SA)

Surface area is the sum of the areas of all the surfaces of a solid. It is measured in square units.

Formulas

❏ 2–dimensional figures

rectangle

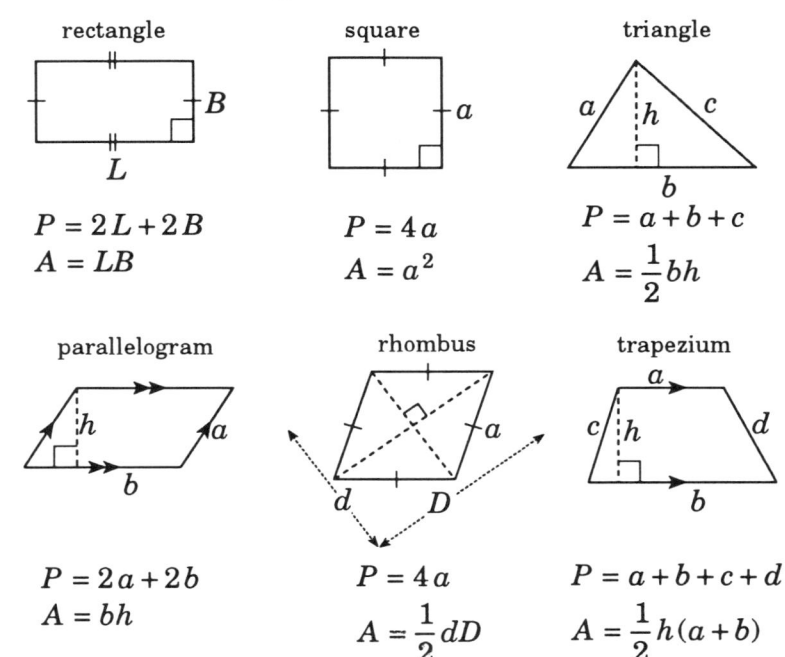

$P = 2L + 2B$
$A = LB$

square

$P = 4a$
$A = a^2$

triangle

$P = a + b + c$
$A = \dfrac{1}{2}bh$

parallelogram

$P = 2a + 2b$
$A = bh$

rhombus

$P = 4a$
$A = \dfrac{1}{2}dD$

trapezium

$P = a + b + c + d$
$A = \dfrac{1}{2}h(a+b)$

kite

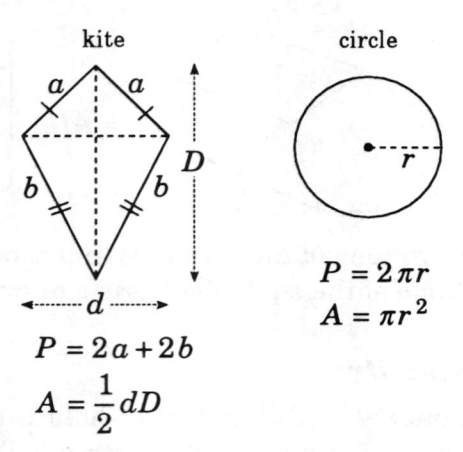

$P = 2a + 2b$
$A = \frac{1}{2}dD$

circle

$P = 2\pi r$
$A = \pi r^2$

❑ 3-dimensional figures

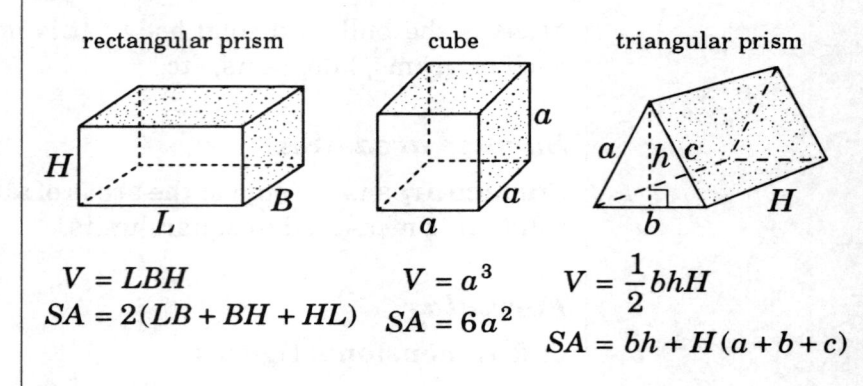

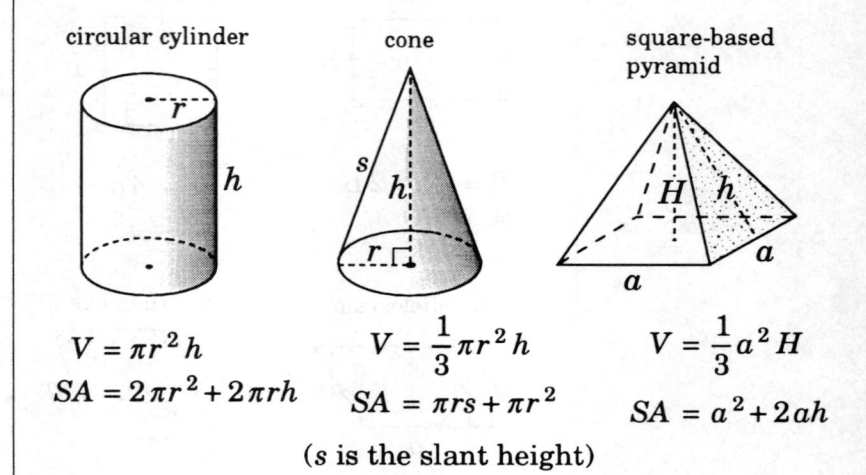

rectangular prism

$V = LBH$
$SA = 2(LB + BH + HL)$

cube

$V = a^3$
$SA = 6a^2$

triangular prism

$V = \frac{1}{2}bhH$
$SA = bh + H(a + b + c)$

circular cylinder

$V = \pi r^2 h$
$SA = 2\pi r^2 + 2\pi rh$

cone

$V = \frac{1}{3}\pi r^2 h$
$SA = \pi rs + \pi r^2$

(s is the slant height)

square-based pyramid

$V = \frac{1}{3}a^2 H$
$SA = a^2 + 2ah$

rectangular-based pyramid

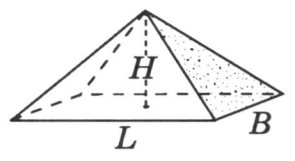

triangular-based pyramid

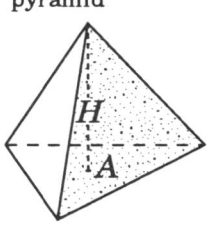

sphere

$$V = \frac{1}{3}LBH$$

$$V = \frac{1}{3}AH$$

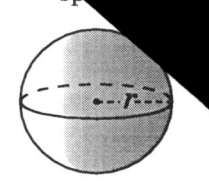

$$V = \frac{4}{3}\pi r^3$$

$$SA = 4\pi r^2$$

Composite figures

❏ **2–dimensional**

$P = \pi r + L + 2B$
$P = 3.14 \times 4 + 8 + 2 \times 5$
$P = 30.56$ cm

$A = \frac{1}{2}\pi r^2 + LB$
$A = \frac{1}{2} \times 3.14 \times 4^2 + 8 \times 5$
$A = 65.12$ cm^2

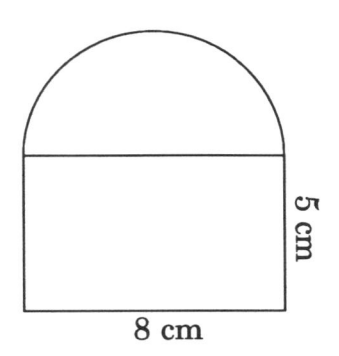

5 cm

8 cm

❏ **3–dimensional**

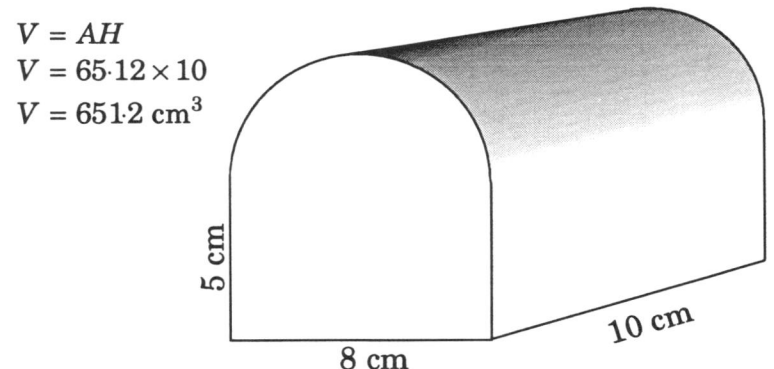

$V = AH$
$V = 65.12 \times 10$
$V = 651.2$ cm^3

5 cm

8 cm

10 cm

SA = ends + base + sides + curved surface
$SA = 65.12 \times 2 + 8 \times 10 + 5 \times 10 \times 2 + 3.14 \times 4 \times 10$
$SA = 435.84$ cm^2

Chapter 5
STATISTICS

This is the study of methods of analysing large quantities of information called **statistics**.

Graphs

Picturegrams

A **picturegram** is a way of representing data in the form of pictures of the objects being represented. One picture may represent only one object or, with large numbers, it may represent many objects, in fact thousands.

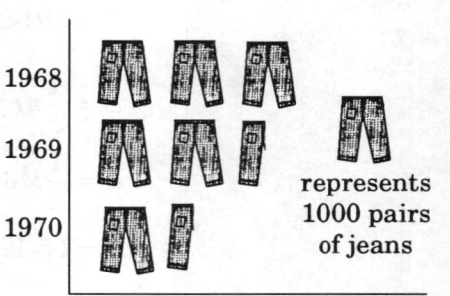

1968
1969
1970

represents 1000 pairs of jeans

Pie charts

A **pie chart** is a circular diagram representing statistical information. The circle is divided into sectors, with the size of the angle at the centre being proportional to the number in that group.

To work out the angle, multiply the percentage by 360°.

Example:
$$30\% = \frac{30}{100} \times 360°$$
$$= 108°$$

To work out the percentage, divide the angle by 360° and multiply by 100%.

Example: $80° = \frac{80}{360} \times 100\% = 22·2\%$

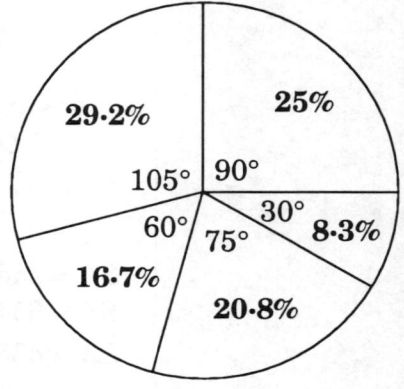

Column graphs

A **column graph** uses vertical columns to represent the number present of each object or group. The columns generally do not touch. In some cases the columns are horizontal. These are called horizontal column graphs or bar graphs. Column graphs are generally used for **discrete data**, such as the number of cars passing a certain intersection, etc.

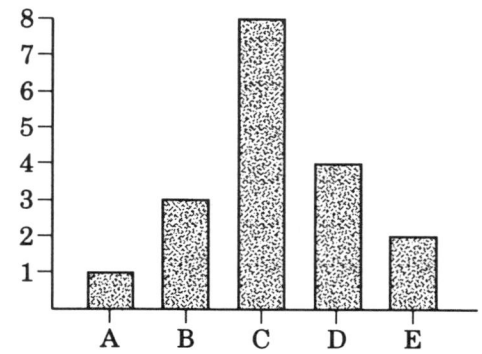

Dot plots

Scores are plotted as 'dots' above the axis.

Example: Construct a dot plot for the following scores:

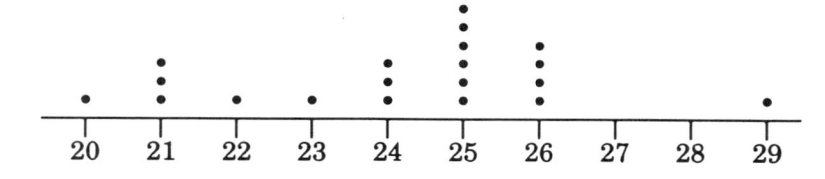

21 23 20 29 25 25 24 26 25 21
22 25 26 24 24 25 26 21 26 25

Stem-and-leaf plots

One part of the score is used as the stem, and the other part forms the leaf.

Example: Construct a stem-and-leaf plot for this data:

57 76 43 57 58 61 69 54 50 45
54 56 42 63 57 51 77 72 48 52
51 59 63 81 39 75 67 58 49 60

the tens digits form the stem

Stem	Leaf
3	9
4	3 5 2 8 9
5	7 7 8 4 0 4 6 7 1 2 1 9 8
6	1 9 3 3 7 0
7	6 7 2 5
8	1

← the units digits form the leaves

← the data shown by this row is 76, 77, 72, 75

Stem-and-leaf plots are usually arranged in order:

```
3 | 9
4 | 2 3 5 8 9
5 | 0 1 1 2 4 4 6 7 7 7 8 8 9
6 | 0 1 3 3 7 9
7 | 2 5 6 7
8 | 1
```

Back-to-back stem-and-leaf plots

Two sets of data can be shown on the same plot.

Example: Jack and Jill sell the following number of milkshakes over 10 days:

Jack   27 13 23 25 7 32 27 44 35 28
Jill   25 18 19 18 32 27 44 35 37 30

```
        Jack    |    Jill
            7   | 0 |
            3   | 1 | 8 8 9
  8 7 7 5 3     | 2 | 5 7
          5 2   | 3 | 0 2 5 7
            4   | 4 | 4
```

Line graphs

When points are plotted to represent the number of data and these points are joined by line segments, a **line graph** is formed. Line graphs are generally used for **continuous data**, such as temperature, time, etc.

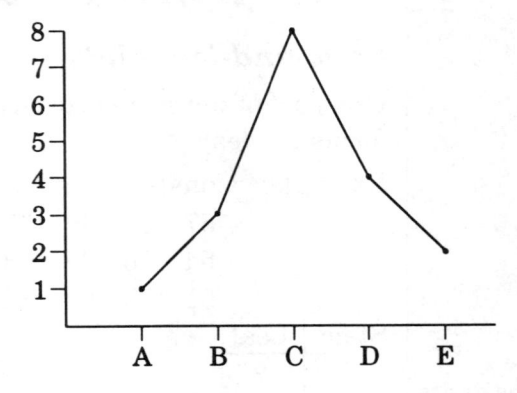

Frequency histograms and polygons

A **frequency histogram** is a column graph where the columns touch half-way between the scores, and the height of each column represents the frequency of that score.

The **frequency polygon** is a line graph formed by joining the midpoint of the top of each column in the frequency histogram.

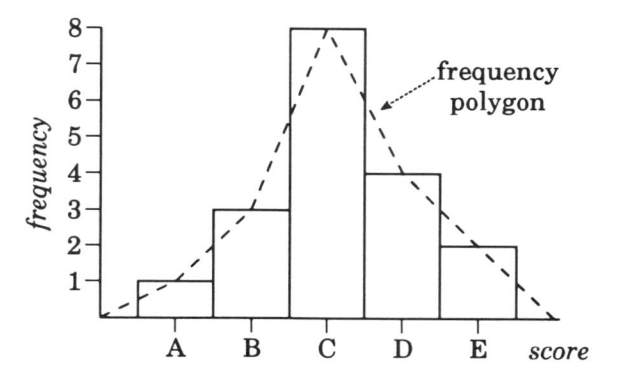

Cumulative frequency histograms and polygons

This is just like the frequency histogram except the heights represent the **cumulative frequency**.

The **cumulative frequency polygon** joins the interior corners of each column of the cumulative frequency histogram.

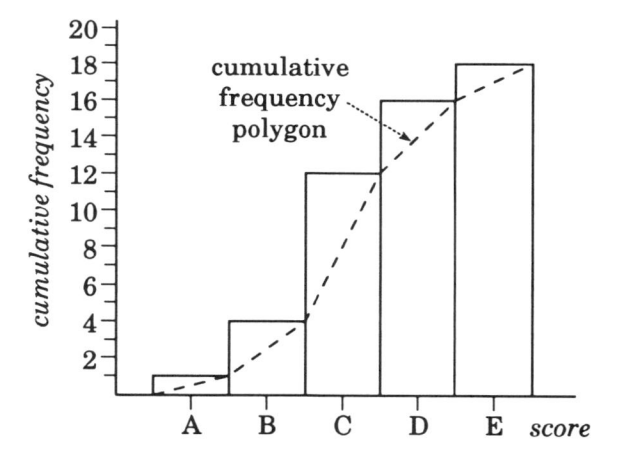

Collecting, sorting and analysing data

Random variable

In general, statistical data are obtained by taking observations or measurements; for example, the number of marks obtained by the students of a class are such observations. The **score**, x, obtained by one student picked at random is a **variable** whose value depends on the student who happens to be picked. The value of x is called the **random variable**, or **variate**.

Frequency (f)

This is the number of times each score occurs in a distribution.

Cumulative frequency (cf)

This is an accumulation of the frequencies. It is found by progressive addition of the frequencies.

Relative frequency (rf)

This is found by dividing each frequency by the sum of the frequencies.

$$rf = \frac{f}{\Sigma f}$$

Distribution tables

16	15	17	11	13	19	20	14	15	18
12	16	15	19	11	14	17	16	16	17
18	12	19	17	16	16	11	18	12	13
16	17	16	18	12	16	15	18	19	17

The above scores can be represented by a frequency distribution table.

Table 1

x	f	fx	cf	rf	$x - \bar{x}$	$f(x - \bar{x})^2$
11	3	33	3	0·075	−4·675	65·567
12	4	48	7	0·1	−3·675	54·023
13	2	26	9	0·05	−2·675	14·311
14	2	28	11	0·05	−1·675	5·611
15	4	60	15	0·1	−0·675	1·823
16	9	144	24	0·225	0·325	0·951
17	6	102	30	0·15	1·325	10·534
18	5	90	35	0·125	2·325	27·028
19	4	76	39	0·1	3·325	44·223
20	1	20	40	0·025	4·325	18·706
Totals	**40**	**627**		**1·0**		**242·777**

$\bar{x}$ is the mean (see next page)

Measures of central tendency

Mode

The **mode** is the most frequently occurring score, that is, it is the **score** with the highest frequency.

In Table 1, **mode = 16**.

Median

The **median** is the middle score. It divides the distribution into two equal parts, in each of which there are an equal number of scores. For example, if there are 35 scores, the middle position is $\frac{1+35}{2} = 18$, i.e. the median is the 18th score.

If there is an even number of scores in the distribution, then the median is the average of the two middle scores. The median need not be an actual score. We can use the cumulative frequency column or the cumulative frequency polygon to find the median. In the above example, the 16th to 24th scores are all 16. The two middle scores, the 20th and the 21st are both 16, so **median = 16**.

Mean ($\bar{x}$)

The mean is the average of all the scores.

$$\bar{x} = \frac{x_1 + x_2 + x_3 + \cdots + x_n}{n} = \frac{\sum x}{n}$$

or

$$\bar{x} = \frac{f_1 x_1 + f_2 x_2 + f_3 x_3 + \cdots + f_r x_r}{n}$$

i.e. $\bar{x} = \frac{\sum fx}{n}$ (where $n = \sum f$)

From the above example, **mean** $\frac{627}{40} = 15.675$.

Measures of dispersion

Range

The range is the difference between the largest and smallest scores, that is,

range = largest score − smallest score

From Table 1, **range = 20 − 11 = 9**.

Deviations from the mean

$x - \bar{x}$ is the deviation of each score from the mean. This measures how far each score is from the mean.

Variance

This is the mean of the squares of the deviations from the mean.

$$V = \frac{\Sigma(x - \bar{x})^2}{n} \quad \text{or} \quad V = \frac{\Sigma f(x - \bar{x})^2}{n}$$

The second formula is used with frequency distribution tables.

From Table 1, $V = \frac{242 \cdot 777}{40}$ 6·069

Mean deviation

This is defined as the mean of the deviations from the mean.

$$\text{mean deviation} = \frac{\Sigma f |x - \bar{x}|}{n} \quad (\text{where } n = \Sigma f)$$

From Table 1, **mean deviation = 2·006**

This measure is generally **not** used by statisticians.

Standard deviation (σ)

This is defined as the square root of the variance. The standard deviation is often referred to as the 'root mean square deviation'.

The standard deviation is given by the formula:

$$\sigma = \sqrt{\frac{\Sigma f(x - \bar{x})^2}{n}} \quad (\text{where } n = \Sigma f)$$

From Table 1, $\sigma = \sqrt{\frac{242 \cdot 777}{40}} = 2 \cdot 4636$.

Using the calculator to find $\bar{x}$ and σ

Place the calculator into statistical mode, then feed in the information. From Table 1:

11 × 3 M+	16 × 9 M+
12 × 4 M+	17 × 6 M+
13 × 2 M+	18 × 5 M+
14 × 2 M+	19 × 4 M+
15 × 4 M+	20 × 1 M+

Then use the statistical keys to find the mean and standard deviation. This varies with calculators.

Consult your calculator handbook or your teacher regarding the correct method for your calculator.

For example, on most Casios:

$$\bar{x} = \boxed{\text{SHIFT}}\ 7 = 15.675$$

$$\sigma = \boxed{\text{SHIFT}}\ 8 = 2.4636$$

Uses of the standard deviation

Normal distribution

A normal distribution has the same value for the mode, the median and the mean, is symmetrical about the mean and is represented by a bell-shaped curve.

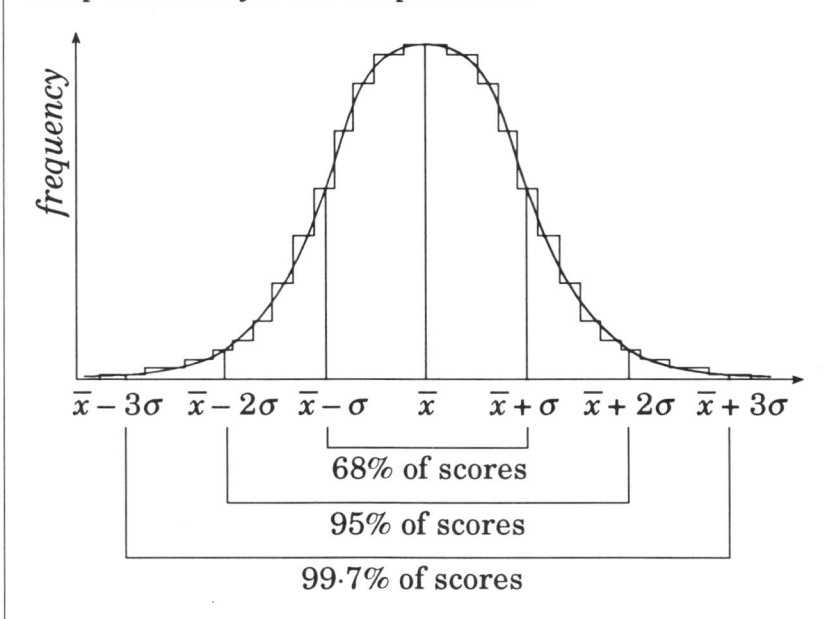

In a normal distribution
- approximately 68% of the scores lie within 1 standard deviation from the mean
- 95% of the scores lie within 2 standard deviations from the mean
- 99·7% of the scores lie within 3 standard deviations from the mean.

In a group of 200 students who sat for a maths exam, the marks awarded were percentages.

If the mean mark was 54 with a standard deviation of 13:

(a) between what marks did 68% of the results lie?

(b) between what marks did 95% of the results lie?

(c) between what marks did 99·7% of the results lie?

Solution:

(a) 68% of the marks lie between 54 ± 13, that is, between 41 and 67.

(b) 95% of the marks lie between $54 \pm 2 \times 13$, that is, between 28 and 80.

(a) 99·7% of the marks lie between $54 \pm 3 \times 13$, that is, between 15 and 93.

Any distribution

For **any** set of scores, the greater the spread, the higher the standard deviation will be.

For most distributions:
- 60% to 70% of the scores will lie within 1 standard deviation from the mean;
- at least 95% of the scores will **very probably** lie within 2 standard deviations from the mean;
- 99·7% of the scores will **almost certainly** lie within 3 standard deviations from the mean.

Interquartile range

If we divide a large distribution into four equal parts, the boundaries between these parts have certain names, known as the **lower quartile**, the **median**, and the **upper quartile**.
- 25% of the scores fall below the **lower quartile**
- 25% of the scores fall above the **upper quartile**
- thus 50% of the scores fall between the lower and the upper quartiles, known as the **interquartile range**.

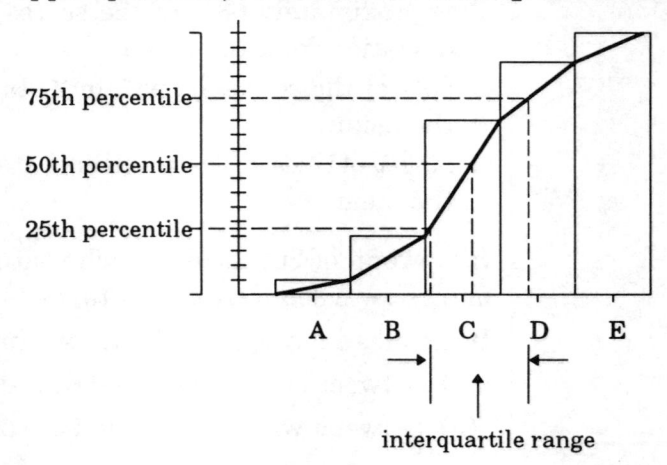

Box-and-whisker plot (or box plot)

The median, the lower quartile, the upper quartile, and the interquartile range can be represented on a diagram called a box-and-whisker plot.

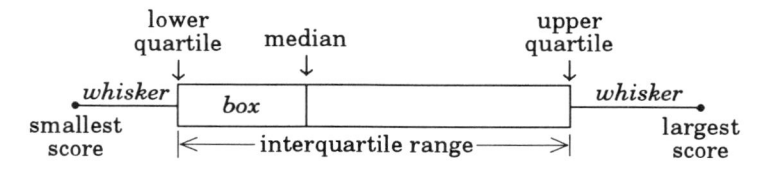

Example: Represent this data in a box-and-whisker plot:

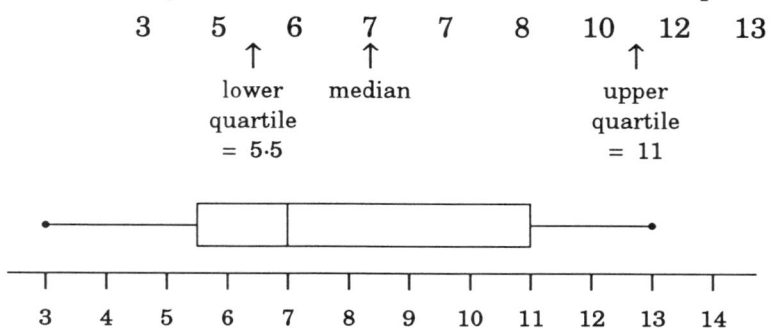

3   5   6   7   7   8   10   12   13

lower quartile = 5·5 (↑ between 5 and 6)

median = 7 (↑)

upper quartile = 11 (↑ between 10 and 12)

Chapter 6
PROBABILITY

This is the study of the likelihood of an event occurring.

Experimental probability

Definition

$$\text{experimental probability} = \frac{\text{number of times this event occurred}}{\text{total number in sample}}$$

$P(E)$ means the probability of event E.

Using relative frequency

From the frequency distribution table on page 56, what is the probability of
- (a) obtaining a score of 16
- (b) obtaining a score ≥ 18

Solution:
- (a) From the table the *rf* of 16 is 0·225
  $\therefore P(16) = 0·225 = 22·5\%$
- (b) From the table the *rf*s of 18, 19 20 are 0·125, 0·1, 0·025
  $\therefore P(\geq 18) = 0·125 + 0·1 + 0·025 = 0·25 = 25\%$

Theoretical probability

Random experiments

A **random experiment** refers to the process of performing an experiment repeatedly in an identical manner without necessarily identical results.

Example: What is the outcome of throwing a die?
Result: 1, 2, 3, 4, 5, 6.

If the experiment is repeated, one of the above results will appear again.

Equally likely outcomes

Outcomes are **equally likely** if there is no reason for one outcome to occur more often than another; for example, when tossing a coin, a head or a tail are equally likely.

Sample space

The sample space is the set of **all** possible outcomes.

Definition of probability

$$P(E) = \frac{\text{number of favourable outcomes}}{\text{number of possible outcomes}}$$

i.e. $P(E) = \dfrac{n(E)}{n(S)}$

where $n(E)$ = number of favourable outcomes of event E and $n(S)$ = number of outcomes of sample space S.

Range of probability

$0 \leq P(E) \leq 1$

If $P(E) = 1$ then the event E is **certain** to occur.
If $P(E) = 0$ then the event E is **impossible**.

Counting techniques

Tree diagrams

The sample space for the tossing of 3 coins or tossing a coin 3 times is:

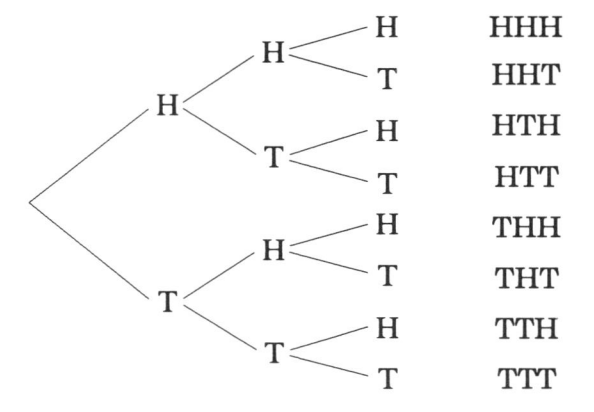

```
        ┌─ H ─┬─ H    HHH
        │     └─ T    HHT
    ┌─ H ┤
    │    │     ┌─ H    HTH
    │    └─ T ─┤
    │          └─ T    HTT
    ┤
    │          ┌─ H    THH
    │    ┌─ H ─┤
    │    │     └─ T    THT
    └─ T ┤
         │     ┌─ H    TTH
         └─ T ─┤
               └─ T    TTT
```

Hence the probability of obtaining two tails and one head is

$$P(2T \text{ and } 1H) = \frac{3}{8}$$

Grid diagrams

Sometimes it is more convenient to represent the sample space by a grid diagram.

Example: Tossing two dice gives the result:

```
1,6   2,6   3,6   4,6   5,6   6,6
1,5   2,5   3,5   4,5   5,5   6,5
1,4   2,4   3,4   4,4   5,4   6,4
1,3   2,3   3,3   4,3   5,3   6,3
1,2   2,2   3,2   4,2   5,2   6,2
1,1   2,1   3,1   4,1   5,1   6,1
```

Thus the probability of throwing a total of 6 is
$$P(6) = \frac{5}{36}$$

Chapter 7
CONSUMER ARITHMETIC

Types of interest

Simple interest

Simple interest is calculated on the principal alone.

The simple interest on P at $r\%$ p.a over t years is given by:
$$I = \frac{Prt}{100}$$

Examples:

1 Find the simple interest on $750 at 5% p.a. over 3 years.
$$I = \frac{750 \times 5 \times 3}{100}$$
$$I = \$112.50$$

2 Find the simple interest on $8200 at 9% p.a. over 5 months.
$$I = \frac{8200 \times 9 \times \frac{5}{12}}{100}$$
$$I = \$307.50$$

3 Find the simple interest on $1250 at 14% p.a. over 150 days.
$$I = \frac{1250 \times 14 \times \frac{150}{365}}{100}$$
$$I = \$71.92$$

Compound interest

Compound interest is calculated on both the principal and its accrued interest; that is, interest is earned by any previous interest.

$$A = P\left(1 + \frac{r}{100}\right)^n$$

P is the principal invested
n is the number of time periods
r is the rate of compound interest for one time period
A is the amount after n time periods

The actual compound interest is found by subtracting the principal from the final amount.

$$CI = A - P$$

CI is the compound interest

Examples:

1. Find what $3500 will amount to in 6 years at 7% p.a. compounded annually.

$$A = 3500\left(1 + \frac{7}{100}\right)^6$$

$$A = \$5252.56$$

2. Find the compound interest on $2000 at 9% p.a over 4 years if interest is compounded six monthly.

The number of periods is 8, and the half-yearly rate of interest is 4·5%.

$$A = 2000\left(1 + \frac{4\cdot5}{100}\right)^8$$

$$A = \$2844.20$$

$$CI = \$2844.20 - \$2000 = \$844.20$$

Purchasing

Depreciation

Depreciation is a reduction in value of something due to its use or age. It is calculated in a similar way to compound interest except the value decreases periodically.

$$V = P\left(1 - \frac{r}{100}\right)^n$$

P is the original value
n is the number of time periods
r is the rate of depreciation for one time period
V is the depreciated amount after n time periods

The depreciation is given by:

$$D = P - V$$

Example:

A car is bought for $48 750 and depreciates at a rate of 17·5% p.a. Find its value after 5 years.

$$V = 48\,750\left(1 - \frac{17\cdot 5}{100}\right)^5$$

$$V = \$18\,631.35$$

Hire purchase

This is a system of buying items such as furniture or white goods, where the buyer pays a deposit and borrows the rest at a certain rate of interest. The balance and the interest are then paid off in equal instalments.

Example:

A stereo colour TV is priced at $2199. After a deposit of $199, the balance incurs simple interest at 11% p.a. over 3 years. If the balance and interest are to be repaid in equal weekly instalments, find the weekly instalment.

$$\text{price} = \$2199$$
$$\text{deposit} = \$199$$
$$\text{balance} = \$2000$$

$$I = \frac{Prt}{100}$$

$$I = \frac{2000 \times 11 \times 3}{100}$$

$$I = \$660$$

Total to be repaid = $2660
Weekly repayment = $2660 ÷ 156 = $17.05

Home loans

This next formula is not required by the syllabus. However, it is an extremely useful formula.

$$M = \frac{Pi}{1 - (1+i)^{-n}}$$

P is the principal borrowed
n is the number of payment periods
i is the rate of interest expressed as a decimal
M is the periodic repayment

Example:

A loan of $120 000 is to be repaid, including interest, over 15 years in equal monthly instalments. If interest is charged at 8·4% p.a. find the monthly repayments.

$$n = 15 \times 12 \text{ months}$$

$$i = \frac{8 \cdot 4}{12 \times 100} = 0 \cdot 007 \quad \left(8 \cdot 4\% \text{ p.a.} = \frac{8 \cdot 4}{12}\% \text{ p.m.}\right)$$

$$M = \frac{120\,000 \times 0 \cdot 007}{1 - (1 \cdot 007)^{-180}}$$

$$= \$1174.66$$

In most cases, tables of loan repayments will be given and calculations become quite simple.

Chapter 8
TRIGONOMETRY

Trigonometry is a branch of mathematics concerned with the measurement of triangles. Unknown angles or lengths of sides of a triangle are calculated by using trigonometrical **ratios** such as **sine**, **cosine**, and **tangent**.

Simple definitions

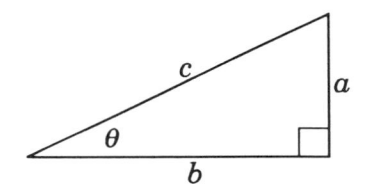

$$\sin \theta = \frac{a}{c}$$

$$\cos \theta = \frac{b}{c}$$

$$\tan \theta = \frac{a}{b}$$

Use of the hand calculator

1 Find $\sin 37°$.
   Calculator is in 'DEG' mode:

     $37\ \boxed{\sin}\ \Rightarrow\ 0.601815023\ \Rightarrow\ 0{\cdot}601\ 815\ 023$

   On a calculator with direct algebraic logic (DAL), the sine function button is pressed first:

     $\boxed{\sin}\ 37\ \Rightarrow\ 0.601815023\ \Rightarrow\ 0{\cdot}601\ 815\ 023$

2 Find $\cos 42° 16'$.

     $42\ \boxed{°\ '\ "}\ 16\ \boxed{°\ '\ "}\ \boxed{\cos}\ \Rightarrow\ 0.740022512$

                                   $\Rightarrow\ 0{\cdot}740\ 022\ 512$

3 Find $\angle A$ to the nearest degree if $\tan A = 1{\cdot}8356$.

     $1{\cdot}8356\ \boxed{\text{SHIFT}}\ \boxed{\tan^{-1}}\ \Rightarrow\ 61.41929119\ \Rightarrow\ 61°$

   On DAL calculators:

     $\boxed{\text{2nd Function}}\ \boxed{\tan^{-1}}\ 1{\cdot}8356\ \Rightarrow\ 61.41929119\ \Rightarrow\ 61°$

4 Find $\angle B$ to the nearest minute if $\sin B = 0{\cdot}37584$.

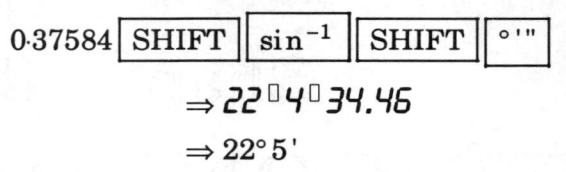

$0{\cdot}37584$ ⎡SHIFT⎤ ⎡$\sin^{-1}$⎤ ⎡SHIFT⎤ ⎡°'"⎤

$\Rightarrow$ *22°4°34.46*

$\Rightarrow 22°5'$

Solving triangles

1 Find the value of x correct to 1 decimal place.

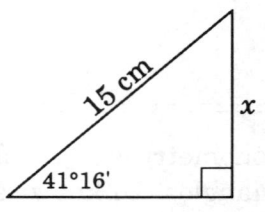

$\sin 41°16' = \dfrac{x}{15}$

$x = 15 \times \sin 41°16'$

$= 15$ ⎡×⎤ 41 ⎡°'"⎤ 16 ⎡°'"⎤ ⎡sin⎤ ⎡=⎤ *9·893467328*

$= 9{\cdot}9$ cm

2 Find the value of h correct to 4 significant figures.

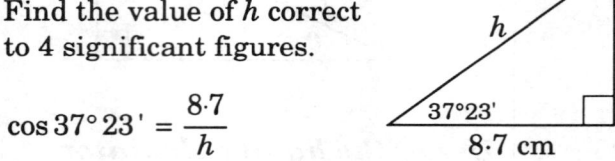

$\cos 37°23' = \dfrac{8{\cdot}7}{h}$

$h = \dfrac{8{\cdot}7}{\cos 37°23'}$

$= 8{\cdot}7$ ⎡÷⎤ 37 ⎡°'"⎤ 23 ⎡°'"⎤ ⎡cos⎤ ⎡=⎤ *10·94902547*

$= 10{\cdot}95$ cm

3 Find θ correct to the nearest minute.

$\tan \theta = \dfrac{8{\cdot}7}{9{\cdot}4}$

$\theta = 8{\cdot}7$ ⎡÷⎤ $9{\cdot}4$ ⎡=⎤ ⎡SHIFT⎤ ⎡$\tan^{-1}$⎤

⎡SHIFT⎤ ⎡°'"⎤ *42°47°6.88*

$= 42°47'$

Angles of elevation and depression

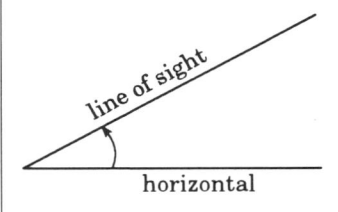

- An **angle of elevation** is the angle between the horizontal and the line of observation when looking *upwards* at an object.

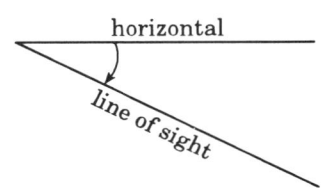

- An **angle of depression** is the angle between the horizontal and the line of observation when looking *downwards* at an object.

New definitions

The trigonometric ratios are redefined as the coordinates of a point on the unit circle.

An angle between the positive x-axis and the other arm of the angle cuts the circle at a point. The coordinates of this point are the cosine and the sine ratio of the angle respectively.

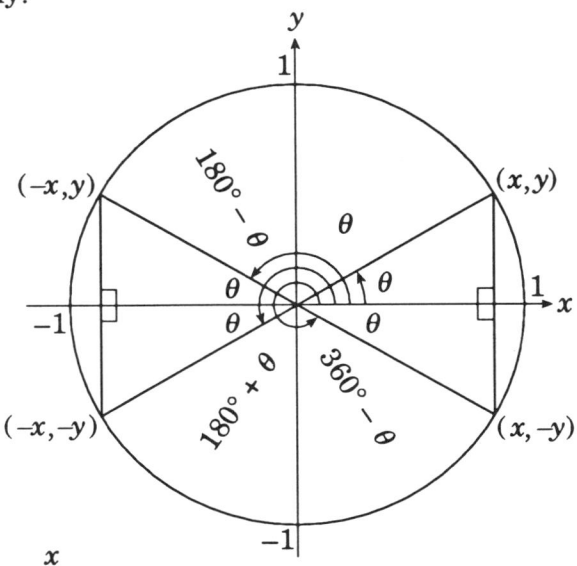

$$\cos \theta = \frac{x}{1} = x$$

$$\sin \theta = \frac{y}{1} = y$$

$$\tan \theta = \frac{y}{x}$$

that is, $(x, y) \equiv (\cos \theta, \sin \theta)$

S	A
T	C

Q1: θ — All are positive
Q2: $180° - \theta$ — Sine is positive
Q3: $180° + \theta$ — Tangent is positive
Q4: $360° - \theta$ — Cosine is positive

Ratios of $-\theta$, $180° \pm \theta$, $360° \pm \theta$ can be expressed in terms of the ratios of θ.

$$\sin(180° - \theta) = \sin\theta \qquad \sin(180° + \theta) = -\sin\theta$$
$$\cos(180° - \theta) = -\cos\theta \qquad \cos(180° + \theta) = -\cos\theta$$
$$\tan(180° - \theta) = -\tan\theta \qquad \tan(180° + \theta) = \tan\theta$$

$$\sin(360° - \theta) = -\sin\theta \qquad \sin(-\theta) = -\sin\theta$$
$$\cos(360° - \theta) = \cos\theta \qquad \cos(-\theta) = \cos\theta$$
$$\tan(360° - \theta) = -\tan\theta \qquad \tan(-\theta) = -\tan\theta$$

The sine rule

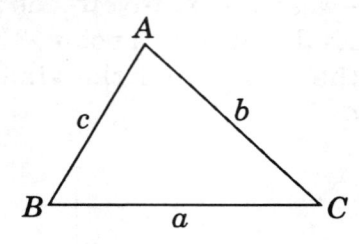

$$\frac{a}{\sin A} = \frac{b}{\sin B} = \frac{c}{\sin C}$$

or

$$\frac{\sin A}{a} = \frac{\sin B}{b} = \frac{\sin C}{c}$$

We use the sine rule
- ❑ to find a side when given two angles and a side
- ❑ to find an angle when given two sides and a non-included angle

Examples:

1 Find x.

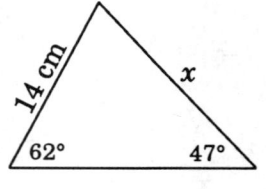

$$\frac{x}{\sin 62°} = \frac{14}{\sin 47°}$$

$$x = \frac{14 \times \sin 62°}{\sin 47°}$$

$$= 16 \cdot 9 \text{ cm}$$

2 Find θ to the nearest minute.

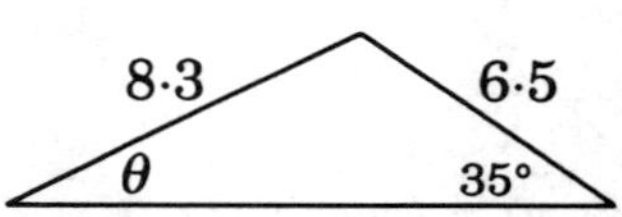

$$\frac{\sin \theta}{6 \cdot 5} = \frac{\sin 35°}{8 \cdot 3}$$

$$\sin \theta = \frac{6 \cdot 5 \times \sin 35°}{8 \cdot 3}$$

$$\theta = 26° \, 41'$$

3 An observer takes a sighting of the top of a mountain and finds the angle of elevation to be 26°. He walks 100 metres closer to the foot of the mountain and finds the angle of elevation to be 31°.

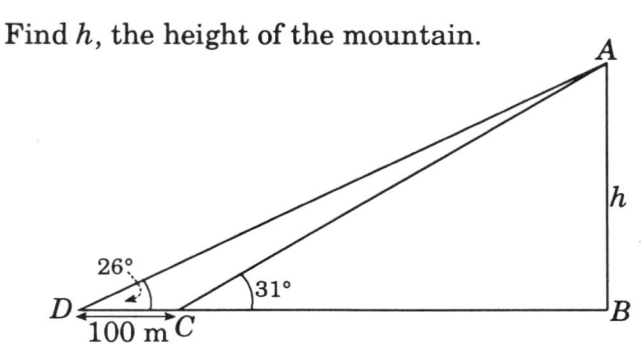

Find h, the height of the mountain.

Let $AC = x$

$\angle DAC = 31° - 26° = 5°$ (ext. $\angle$ of $\triangle$ thm.)

By the sine rule: $\dfrac{x}{\sin 26°} = \dfrac{100}{\sin 5°}$

$$x = \dfrac{100 \sin 26°}{\sin 5°}$$

From $\triangle ABC$: $\dfrac{h}{x} = \sin 31°$

$h = x \sin 31°$

$= \dfrac{100 \sin 26° \sin 31°}{\sin 5°}$

$= 259$ metres

The cosine rule

$$a^2 = b^2 + c^2 - 2bc \cos A$$

or

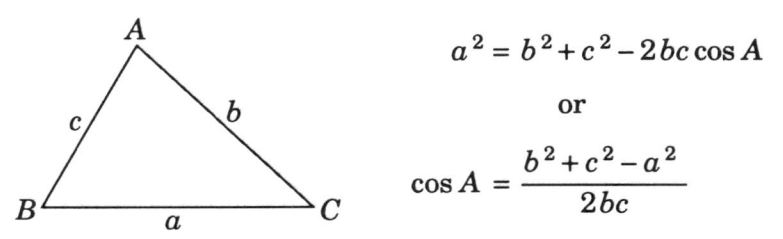

$$\cos A = \dfrac{b^2 + c^2 - a^2}{2bc}$$

We use the cosine rule:
- to find a side when given two sides and the included angle
- to find an angle when given three sides.

Examples:

1 Find x.

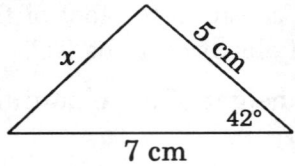

$$x^2 = 7^2 + 5^2 - 2 \times 7 \times 5 \cos 42°$$
$$x = 4.69 \text{ cm}$$

2 Find θ to the nearest degree.

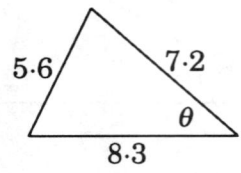

$$\cos \theta = \frac{8.3^2 + 7.2^2 - 5.6^2}{2 \times 8.3 \times 7.2}$$
$$\theta = 42°$$

Area of a triangle

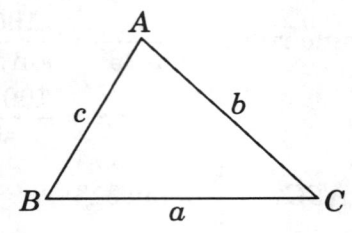

$$\text{area} = \frac{1}{2} bc \sin A$$
$$\text{area} = \frac{1}{2} ca \sin B$$
$$\text{area} = \frac{1}{2} ab \sin C$$

that is, area = $\frac{1}{2} \times \begin{pmatrix} \text{product} \\ \text{of 2 sides} \end{pmatrix} \times \begin{pmatrix} \text{sine of the} \\ \text{included angle} \end{pmatrix}$

Example:

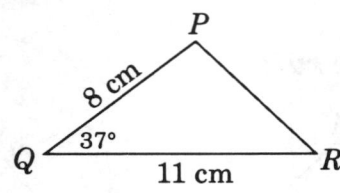

Find the area of $\triangle PQR$.

$$\text{area} = \frac{1}{2} \times 8 \times 11 \times \sin 37°$$
$$= 26.5 \text{ cm}^2$$

Chapter 9
COORDINATE GEOMETRY

This is a system of geometry using an ordered pair of numbers as coordinates to locate points on a plane or in space.

Number plane

The **number plane** is formed by two axes, usually the ***x*-axis** (horizontal) and the ***y*-axis** (vertical). Points are located by using two numbers separated by a comma and written in parentheses. The ***x*-coordinate** is always written before the ***y*-coordinate**. The point of intersection of the two axes is called the **origin**.

Plotting points

(1, 3) is called an **ordered pair** or the **coordinates of a point**. The first number is the reading on the *x*-axis, that is, how far right or left. The second number is the reading on the *y*-axis, that is, how far up or down.

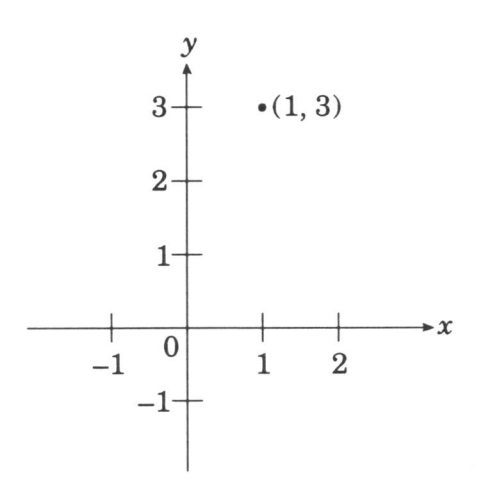

Graphs of lines

Example: Graph the lines $y = x+1$, $2x+3y = 6$.
Find the intercepts on the axes, that is, when $x = 0$ and $y = 0$.

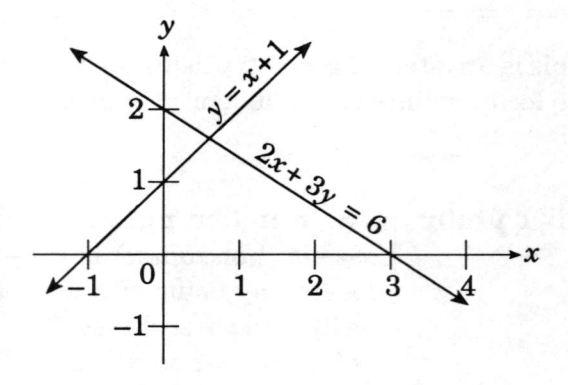

$$y = x+1 \qquad\qquad 2x+3y = 6$$
$$x = 0 \implies y = 1 \qquad\qquad x = 0 \implies y = 2$$
$$y = 0 \implies x = -1 \qquad\qquad y = 0 \implies x = 3$$

Travel graphs

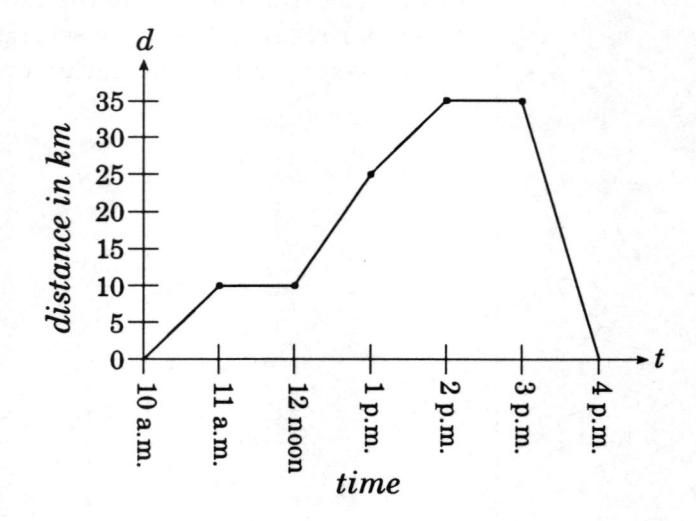

Conversion graphs

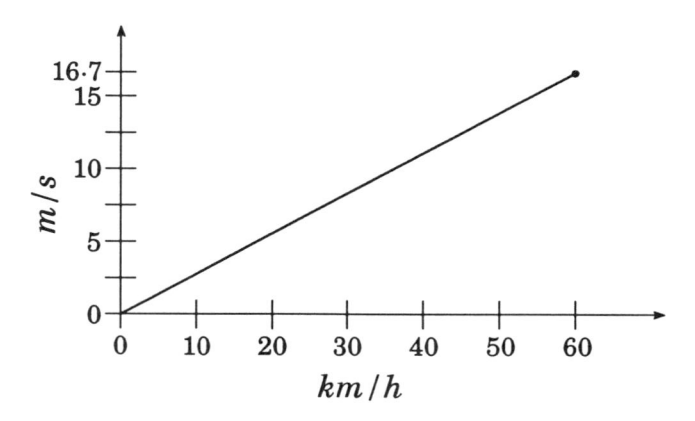

Curves

Of the form $y = x^n$

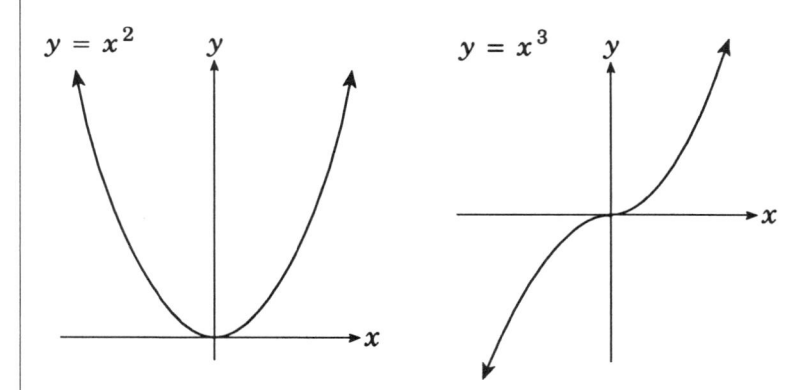

$y = x^2$

$y = x^3$

Rectangular hyperbola

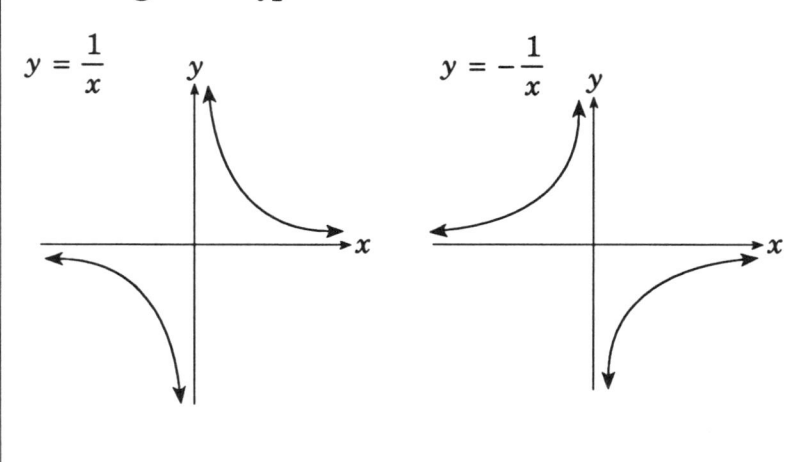

$y = \dfrac{1}{x}$

$y = -\dfrac{1}{x}$

Distance, gradient, and midpoint

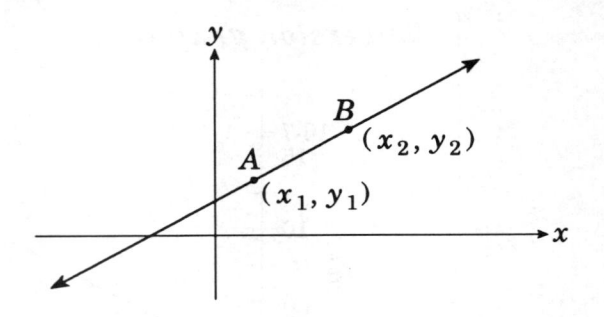

Distance between two points
The distance AB is given by $d = \sqrt{(x_2-x_1)^2+(y_2-y_1)^2}$.

Gradient of interval joining two points
The gradient of AB is given by $m = \dfrac{y_2-y_1}{x_2-x_1}$.

Midpoint of an interval
The midpoint of AB is given by $x = \dfrac{x_1+x_2}{2}$, $y = \dfrac{y_1+y_2}{2}$.

Example: Find the distance, gradient, and midpoint of the interval joining the points, $(-1, 3)$ and $(5, 8)$.

$$d = \sqrt{(5-(-1))^2 + (8-3)^2}$$
$$= \sqrt{36+25}$$
$$= \sqrt{61}$$

Hence the distance is $\sqrt{61}$ units.

$$m = \frac{8-3}{5-(-1)}$$
$$= \frac{5}{6}$$

Hence the gradient is $\dfrac{5}{6}$.

$$x = \frac{-1+5}{2}, \quad y = \frac{3+8}{2}$$
$$x = 2, \quad y = 5\tfrac{1}{2}$$

Hence the midpoint is $\left(2, 5\tfrac{1}{2}\right)$.

Equations of straight lines

General form
$$Ax + By + C = 0$$

Gradient–intercept form

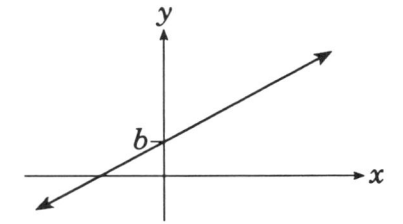

Given the gradient m and the y-intercept b, the equation is
$$y = mx + b.$$

Example: The equation of the line with gradient 4 and y-intercept 3 is $y = 4x + 3$.

Point–gradient form

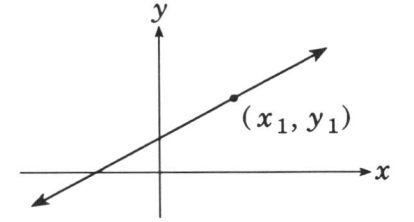

Given the gradient m and a point (x_1, y_1) on it, the equation is
$$y - y_1 = m(x - x_1).$$

Example: The equation of the line with gradient -2 and passing through the point $(3, 7)$ is
$$y - 7 = -2(x - 3)$$
$$2x + y - 13 = 0$$

Two-point form
Given two points (x_1, y_1) and (x_2, y_2) the equation is
$$\frac{y - y_1}{x - x_1} = \frac{y_2 - y_1}{x_2 - x_1}.$$

There is no need to learn this formula because you can always use the gradient formula to find m and then use the point–gradient form of a line to find its equation.

Gradient of the general form

For the line $Ax + By + C = 0$, the gradient is given by

$$m = -\frac{A}{B}.$$

Example: Find the gradient of the line $5x - 4y + 9 = 0$.

$$m = -\frac{5}{-4} = \frac{5}{4}$$

Parallel and perpendicular lines

Parallel lines

The condition for two lines to be parallel is that their gradients are equal, that is, $m_1 = m_2$.

Example: Find the equation of the line parallel to
$$3x + 5y - 7 = 0$$
and passing through the point $(-2, 4)$.

Gradient of given line is $-\frac{3}{5}$, so the gradient of the parallel line is also $-\frac{3}{5}$.

Using $y - y_1 = m(x - x_1)$, the parallel line will be:
$$y - 4 = -\frac{3}{5}(x - (-2))$$
$$5(y - 4) = -3(x + 2)$$
$$5y - 20 = -3x - 6$$
$$3x + 5y - 14 = 0$$

Perpendicular lines

The condition for two lines to be perpendicular is that the product of their gradients is -1, that is,

$$m_1 m_2 = -1 \quad \text{or} \quad m_1 = -\frac{1}{m_2}.$$

The gradients of perpendicular lines are negative reciprocals of each other.

Example: Find the equation of the line perpendicular to
$$3x + 5y - 7 = 0$$
and passing through the point $(-2, 4)$.

Gradient of given line is $-\dfrac{3}{5}$,

so the gradient of the perpendicular line is $\dfrac{5}{3}$.

Using $y - y_1 = m(x - x_1)$, the perpendicular line will be:
$$y - 4 = \dfrac{5}{3}(x - (-2))$$
$$3(y - 4) = 5(x + 2)$$
$$3y - 12 = 5x + 10$$
$$5x - 3y + 22 = 0$$

Chapter 10
FUNCTIONS & MAPPING

Definitions
- A **relation** is a set of ordered pairs. The two elements are often matched by some rule.
- A **function** is a set of ordered pairs in which no two pairs have the same first element.

Hence, a function is a special relation, but a relation need not be a function.

Vertical line test
Any vertical line will cut a function at only one point, but will cut a non-function relation at more than one point.

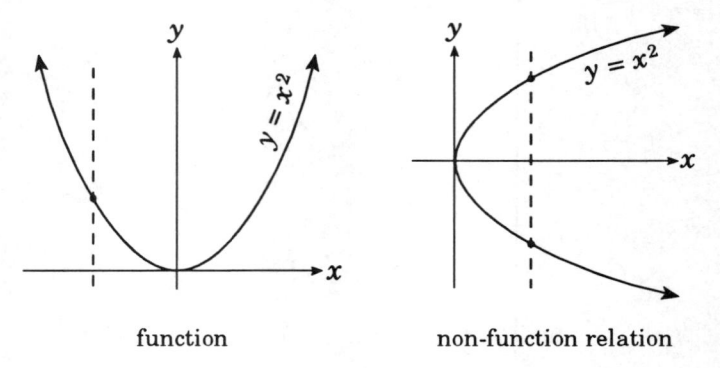

function   non-function relation

Domain and range
In any function or relation
- the set of *first* elements is called the **domain**
- the set of *second* elements is called the **range**.

Example:

For the relation $\{(1, 2), (2, 3), (3, 4), (4, 5), (5, 6)\}$

$$\text{the domain} = \{1, 2, 3, 4, 5\}$$
$$\text{the range} = \{2, 3, 4, 5, 6\}$$

For the function $y = x^2$

the domain is all real values of x

the range is $y \geq 0$

Function notation

There are many notations to represent a mapping of a member of the domain X to a member of the range Y.

For example, $h: X \to Y$ or $X \xrightarrow{h} Y$

These are: the function h maps the set X to the set Y

The more common notations are

$\quad\quad x \to h(x) \quad$ (for example, $h: x \to 2x^3$)

or $\quad y = h(x) \quad$ (for example, $h(x) = 2x^3$)

Examples:

1 If $h: x \to 2x^3$, complete the ordered pairs

$$(1, \ ), (2, \ ), (3, \ ), (7, \ )$$

Solution:
$$1 \to 2 \times 1^3 \quad \to 2$$
$$2 \to 2 \times 2^3 \quad \to 16$$
$$3 \to 2 \times 3^3 \quad \to 54$$
$$7 \to 2 \times 7^3 \quad \to 686$$

So the ordered pairs are $(1, 2), (2, 16), (3, 54), (7, 686)$.

2 If $f(x) = 3x - 4$, find $f(0), f(2), f(-1), f\left(\frac{1}{3}\right)$

Solution:
$$f(x) = 3x - 4$$
$$f(0) = 3 \times 0 - 4 \quad = -4$$
$$f(2) = 3 \times 2 - 4 \quad = 2$$
$$f(-1) = 3 \times (-1) - 4 = -7$$
$$f\left(\tfrac{1}{3}\right) = 3 \times \tfrac{1}{3} - 4 \quad = -3$$

Two-variable mappings

This is when a set of points on the number plane is mapped to another set of points on the number plane.

Example:

The mapping, $g: (x, y) \rightarrow (x+1, y+3)$, shifts all the points in the number plane 1 unit to the right and 3 units up.

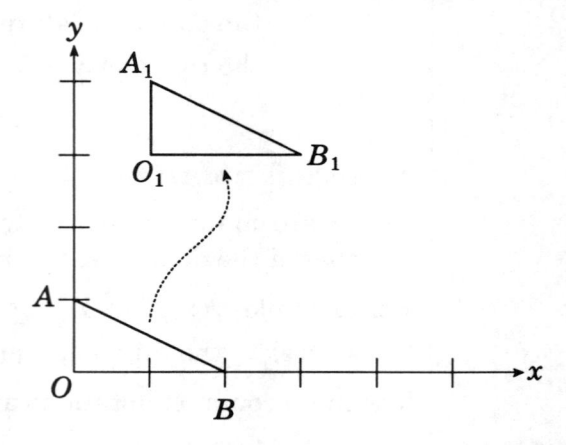

Under this mapping, $\triangle OAB$ is moved to $\triangle O_1 A_1 B_1$,
where
$$O(0, 0) \rightarrow O_1(1, 3)$$
$$A(0, 1) \rightarrow A_1(1, 4)$$
$$B(2, 0) \rightarrow B_1(3, 3)$$

Transformations

Translations

A translation shifts ordered pairs in a line, that is
$$t: (x, y) \rightarrow (x+p, y+q)$$

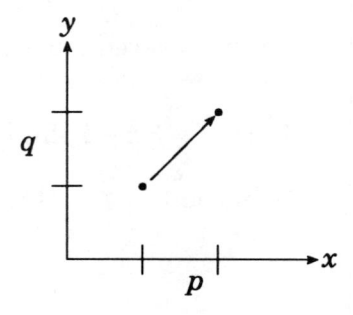

Reflections

A reflection flips ordered pairs as mirror images in a line.

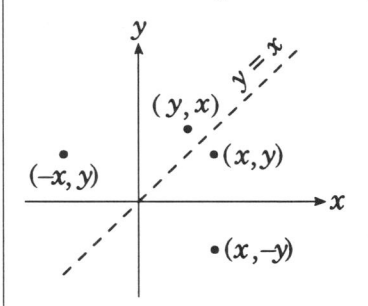

$r_x: (x, y) \to (x, -y)$
reflects in the x axis

$r_y: (x, y) \to (-x, y)$
reflects in the y axis

$r_{(y=x)}: (x, y) \to (y, x)$
reflects in the line $y = x$

Rotations

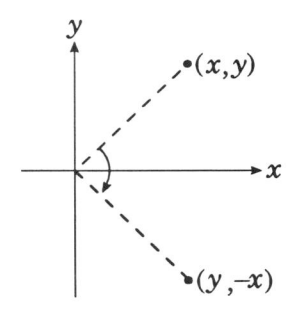

A rotation spins the set of ordered pairs about a fixed point through a given angle.

$R_{90°}: (x, y) \to (y, -x)$
rotates in a clockwise direction through an angle of 90°.

Composite mappings

These occur when one mapping is followed by another mapping.

- $f[g(x)]$ means mapping g is followed by mapping f
- $g[f(x)]$ means mapping f is followed by mapping g
- $f[f(x)]$ or $f^2(x)$ means mapping f is followed by mapping f again.

Example:

If $f: (x, y) \to (x+2, -y)$ $g: (x, y) \to (-x-1, y+1)$,
find $f[g(1, 2)]$, $g[f(1, 2)]$, $f^2(1, 2)$.

Solution: $g(1, 2) = (-2, 3) \Rightarrow f(-2, 3) = (0, -3)$
∴ $f[g(1, 2)] = (0, -3)$

$f(1, 2) = (3, -2) \Rightarrow g(3, -2) = (-4, -1)$
∴ $g[f(1, 2)] = (-4, -1)$

$f(1, 2) = (3, -2) \Rightarrow f(3, -2) = (5, 2)$
∴ $f^2(1, 2) = (5, 2)$

In general, $g(x, y) = (-x - 1, y + 1)$ followed by f
$$\Rightarrow f(-x - 1, y + 1) = (-x + 1, -y - 1)$$
$$\therefore f[g(x, y)] = (-x + 1, -y - 1)$$
$f(x, y) = (x + 2, -y)$ followed by g
$$\Rightarrow g(x + 2, -y) = (-x - 3, -y + 1)$$
$$\therefore g[f(x, y)] = (-x - 3, -y + 1)$$

Composite functions (or function of a function)

The composition of two functions, $y = f(x)$ and $y = g(x)$ is given by $y = f[g(x)]$.

The g is called the inner function and the f is called the outer function.

If $f(x) = x^2$, $g(x) = 3x - 2$, then
$$f[g(x)] = (3x - 2)^2$$
$$g[f(x)] = 3x^2 - 2$$

Inverse functions

Since a function maps each element of the domain to a single element of the range, an **inverse mapping**, if it can be found, will map that element of the range back to the element of the domain. The inverse of a function might not be a function.

If the original function is denoted by f, then the inverse mapping (or inverse function) is denoted by f^{-1}.

Any mapping which maps an element back onto itself is called an **identity mapping**.

Hence $f^{-1}[f(x)] = f[f^{-1}(x)] = I(x) = x$.

Finding the inverse function

A function and its **inverse relation** are mirror images of each other in the line $y = x$.

To find the inverse relation of $y = f(x)$, first interchange x and y and then make y the subject. If there is only one value of y for each value of x, then the inverse is a function.

Examples:

1. Find the inverse function of $y = 3x - 2$.

   Solution:
   $$y = 3x - 2$$
   $$x = 3y - 2 \quad \text{(interchanging } x \text{ and } y\text{)}$$
   $$x + 2 = 3y \quad \text{(changing the subject to } y\text{)}$$
   $$\therefore \quad y = \frac{x+2}{3}$$

   $\therefore$ the inverse function is $y = \dfrac{x+2}{3}$

2. Find the inverse function of $y = \dfrac{5x+4}{x-2}$.

   Solution:
   $$y = \frac{5x+4}{x-2}$$
   $$x = \frac{5y+4}{y-2} \quad \text{(interchanging } x \text{ and } y\text{)}$$
   $$x(y-2) = 5y + 4 \quad \text{(changing the subject to } y\text{)}$$
   $$xy - 2x = 5y + 4$$
   $$xy - 5y = 2x + 4$$
   $$y(x-5) = 2x + 4$$
   $$\therefore \quad y = \frac{2x+4}{x-5}$$

   $\therefore$ the inverse function is $y = \dfrac{2x+4}{x-5}$

Chapter 11
THEORY OF LOGARITHMS

Simple exponential equations

An exponential equation is one where the pronumeral to be solved is involved in the *exponent* or *index*.

Examples:
$$2^x = 32 \qquad 5^{2x-1} = 125$$

Solutions:
$$2^x = 32 \qquad 5^{2x-1} = 125$$
$$2^x = 2^5 \qquad 5^{2x-1} = 5^3$$
$$\therefore \quad x = 5 \qquad \therefore \quad 2x - 1 = 3$$
$$\therefore \quad x = 2$$

Definition

If a positive number M is expressed in the form $M = a^x$ then the index x is the logarithm of the number M to the base a, written as $x = \log_a M$.

Thus $M = a^x$ and $x = \log_a M$ are equivalent statements.

Logarithmic and exponential graphs

Graphs of $y = a^x$ and $y = \log_a x$:

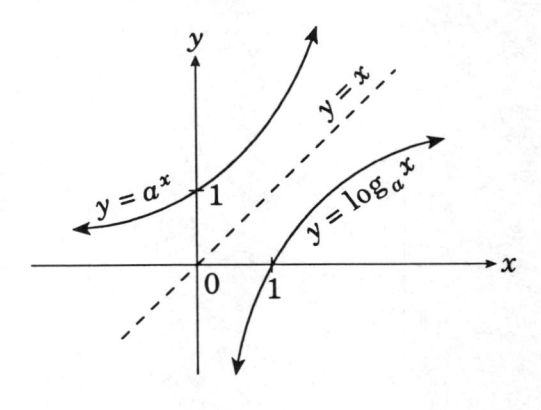

The curves are reflections of each other in the line $y = x$, clearly indicating that they are inverse functions.

Laws of logarithms

1. $\log_a MN = \log_a M + \log_a N$
2. $\log_a \dfrac{M}{N} = \log_a M - \log_a N$
3. $\log_a M^p = p \log_a M$
4. $\log_a M = \dfrac{\log_b M}{\log_b a}$ (change of base law)
5. $\log_a a = 1$ $(a > 0)$
6. $\log_a 1 = 0$ $(a \neq 0)$

Examples:

1. Simplify $\log_{10} 125 + \log_{10} 8$.

   Solution:
   $$\begin{aligned}
   \log_{10} 125 + \log_{10} 8 &= \log_{10}(125 \times 8) \\
   &= \log_{10} 1000 \\
   &= \log_{10} 10^3 \\
   &= 3 \log_{10} 10 \\
   &= 3
   \end{aligned}$$

2. Simplify $\dfrac{\log_b x^5}{\log_b \sqrt[3]{x}}$

   Solution:
   $$\begin{aligned}
   \dfrac{\log_b x^5}{\log_b \sqrt[3]{x}} &= \dfrac{\log_b x^5}{\log_b x^{\frac{1}{3}}} \\
   &= \dfrac{5 \log_b x}{\frac{1}{3} \log_b x} \\
   &= 15
   \end{aligned}$$

3 In the expression $2\log x - \log y = \log 4$ find a relationship between x and y, not involving logarithms.

Solution:
$$2\log x - \log y = \log 4$$
$$\log x^2 - \log y = \log 4$$
$$\log\left(\frac{x^2}{y}\right) = \log 4$$
$$\therefore \quad \frac{x^2}{y} = 4$$
$$\therefore \quad x^2 = 4y$$

4 Solve for x the equation $3^x = 15$.

Solution:
$$3^x = 15$$
$$x = \log_3 15$$
$$= \frac{\log_{10} 15}{\log_{10} 3}$$
$$= \frac{1.176091259}{0.477121254} \quad \text{(using a calculator)}$$
$$= 2.464\ 97$$

Chapter 12
POLYNOMIALS

A **polynomial** is an algebraic expression containing the sum or difference of many terms, where each term is made up of the product of a number and a non-negative power of a variable such as x.

Notation

The notation for a polynomial is $P(x)$.

$P(x)$ can be written in the form

$$P(x) = a_n x^n + a_{n-1} x^{n-1} + \ldots + a_2 x^2 + a_1 x^1 + a_0 x^0$$

$a_n, a_{n-1}, \ldots a_2, a_1, a_0$ are the coefficients of x

$a_n x^n$ is the leading term

n is the degree of the polynomial (if $a_n \neq 0$)

a_n is the leading coefficient

a_0 is the constant term (since $x^0 = 1$)

Example:

$$P(x) = 3x^4 + 5x^3 - 7x^2 + 2x - 11$$

degree = 4
constant = 11
leading coefficient = 3
coefficient of x^2 = -7
number of terms = 5

If the degree of the polynomial is 1 (such as $x - 3$), then it is a **linear polynomial**.

Addition and subtraction

When adding or subtracting polynomials, collect like terms, (that is, like powers of the variable).

Examples:

$(7x^2+5x-4)+(2x^3-3x^2+x+7) = 2x^3+4x^2+6x+3$

$(5x^4-3x^2-11x+4)-(4x^3-8x^2-x+7)$
$= 5x^4-4x^3-3x^2-(-8x^2)-11x-(-x)+4-7$
$= 5x^4-4x^3+5x^2-10x-3$

Multiplication

Each term in the second set of brackets is multiplied by each term in the first set of brackets.

Examples:

$(x+3)(2x^2-5x+7)$
$= x(2x^2-5x+7)+3(2x^2-5x+7)$
$= 2x^3-5x^2+7x+6x^2-15x+21$
$= 2x^3+x^2-8x+21$

$(3x^2-4x+2)(x^4+5x-3)$
$= 3x^2(x^4+5x-3)-4x(x^4+5x-3)+2(x^4+5x-3)$
$= 3x^6+15x^3-9x^2-4x^5-20x^2+12x+2x^4+10x-6$
$= 3x^6-4x^5+2x^4+15x^3-29x^2+22x-6$

Division

Example:

$$\begin{array}{r} 3x^3+x^2+6x+11 \\ x-2{\overline{\smash{\big)}\,3x^4-5x^3+4x^2-x-3}} \\ \underline{3x^4-6x^3} \\ x^3 \\ \underline{x^3-2x^2} \\ 6x^2 \\ \underline{6x^2-12x} \\ 11x \\ \underline{11x-22} \\ 19 \end{array}$$

The result may be written as

$$\underbrace{3x^4 - 5x^3 + 4x^2 - x - 3}_{\text{dividend}} = \underbrace{(x-2)}_{\text{divisor}}\underbrace{(3x^3 + x^2 + 6x - 13)}_{\text{quotient}} \underbrace{- 29}_{\text{remainder}}$$

In general, if $P(x)$ is divided by $A(x)$, giving a quotient $Q(x)$ and remainder $R(x)$ then the result can be written as
$$P(x) = A(x) \cdot Q(x) + R(x)$$

The remainder theorem

If $A(x)$ is a linear polynomial $x - a$, then the remainder must be a constant, say r,

$\therefore \quad P(x) = (x-a) \cdot Q(x) + r$

Now, if we let $x = a$, then $P(a) = (a-a) \cdot Q(a) + r$

i.e. $P(a) = 0 \cdot Q(a) + r$

$\therefore \quad P(a) = r$

Thus, when a polynomial $P(x)$ is divided by $(x - a)$, the remainder is $P(a)$.

Examples:

Find the remainder when:

1. $2x^3 - 5x^2 + 7x + 2$ is divided by $x - 3$
2. $x^4 + 2x^3 - 8x^2 - 11x - 5$ is divided by $x + 1$

Solutions:

1. $P(3) = 2(3)^3 - 5(3)^2 + 7(3) + 2 = 32$
   $\therefore$ remainder = 32

2. $P(-1) = (-1)^4 + 2(-1)^3 - 8(-1)^2 - 11(-1) - 5 = -3$
   $\therefore$ remainder = -3

The factor theorem

For a divisor to be a factor, the remainder must be zero,
$\therefore (x - a)$ is a factor of $P(x)$ if and only if $P(a) = 0$.

Examples:

1. Show that $x + 2$ is a factor of $x^3 - 2x^2 - 5x + 6$.
   $P(-2) = (-2)^3 - 2(-2)^2 - 5(-2) + 6$
   $\quad\quad = -8 - 8 + 10 + 6$
   $\quad\quad = 0$
   $\therefore \; x + 2$ is a factor

2 Find the factors of $x^3 + 4x^2 - 15x - 18$.

Try $x = -1$: $P(-1) = -1 + 4 + 15 - 18 = 0$

$\therefore$ $x + 1$ is a factor

Try $x = -2$: $P(-2) = -8 + 16 + 30 - 18 \neq 0$

Try $x = 3$: $P(3) = 27 + 36 - 45 - 18 = 0$

$\therefore$ $x - 3$ is another factor

Since $-18 = (-1) \times 3 \times 6$, the remaining factor must be $x + 6$, $\therefore$ the factorised form is $(x + 1)(x - 3)(x + 6)$.

Graphs of polynomial functions

If the polynomial has an **even** degree, then the 'arrows' at the ends of the curve will point in the **same** direction.

If the leading coefficient is **positive** then the 'arrows' point **upwards**.

If the leading coefficient is **negative** then the 'arrows' point **downwards**.

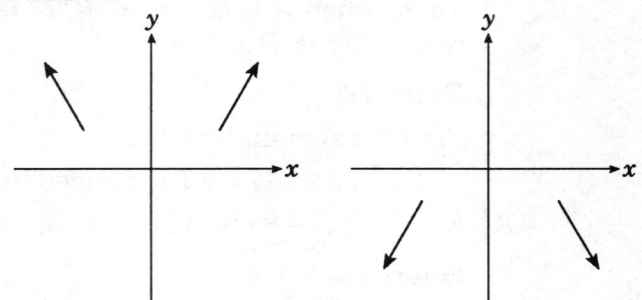

If the polynomial has an odd degree, then the 'arrows' at the ends of the curve will point in the **opposite** direction.

If the leading coefficient is **positive** then the 'left arrow' points **downwards**.

If the leading coefficient is **negative** then the 'left arrow' point **upwards**.

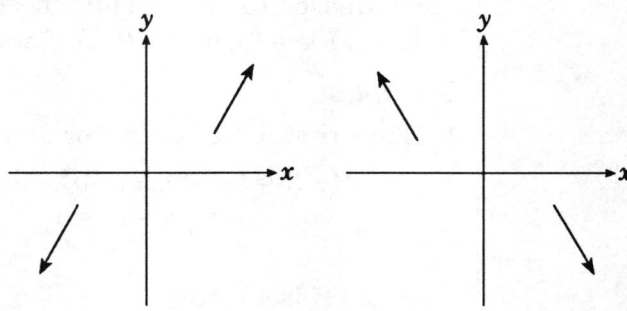

Examples:

1 The sketch of $y = (x+3)(x-1)(x-2)$ is:

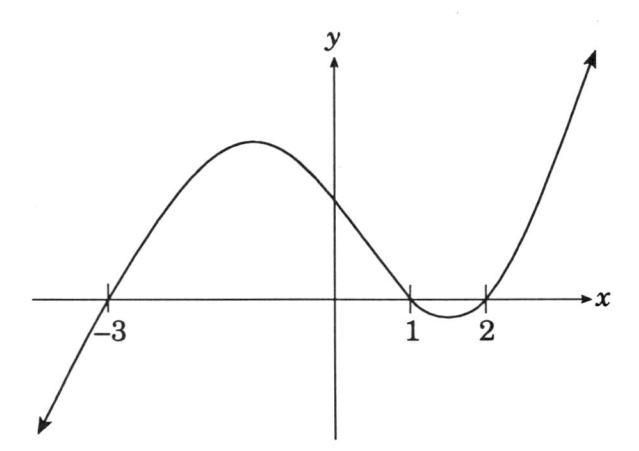

2 The sketch of $y = (x+4)(x+1)(x-2)(x-3)$ is:

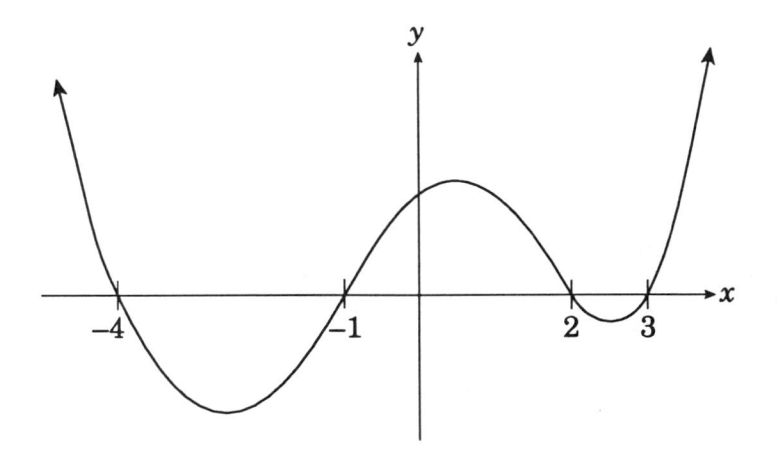

Chapter 13
MATRICES & TRANSFORMATIONS

Definitions

- A **matrix** is a rectangular array of elements enclosed by square brackets. If the matrix has m **rows** and n **columns** the **order** of the matrix is $m \times n$. It is said to be an $m \times n$ matrix.

  Note that the number of rows is mentioned first.

  Examples: $\begin{bmatrix} 5 & 2 \\ 3 & 7 \\ 1 & 4 \end{bmatrix}$ This is a 3×2 matrix.

  $\begin{bmatrix} 5 & 3 & 1 \\ 2 & 7 & 4 \end{bmatrix}$ This is a 2×3 matrix.

- Matrices that have the same number of rows and columns are called **square matrices**.

  If the matrix is square, then it has two diagonals, and the one from the top-left corner to the bottom-right corner is the **principal** or **leading diagonal** or **axis**.

  $\begin{bmatrix} 5 & 2 & 7 \\ 8 & 6 & 4 \\ 1 & 0 & 3 \end{bmatrix}$

- For a square matrix, if one side of the principal axis is a reflection of the other, then the matrix is said to be a **symmetric matrix**.

  $\begin{bmatrix} 5 & 2 & 7 \\ 2 & 6 & 4 \\ 7 & 4 & 3 \end{bmatrix}$ Note that for a symmetric matrix the rows and columns can be interchanged without altering the matrix.

Addition of matrices

❏ The addition of two matrices is obtained by adding corresponding elements of each matrix.

If $\mathbf{A} = \begin{bmatrix} a & b \\ c & d \end{bmatrix} \quad \mathbf{B} = \begin{bmatrix} e & f \\ g & h \end{bmatrix}$

$\mathbf{A} + \mathbf{B} = \begin{bmatrix} a+e & b+f \\ c+g & d+h \end{bmatrix}$

Example:

$\begin{bmatrix} 2 & 5 \\ -1 & 3 \end{bmatrix} + \begin{bmatrix} 3 & 4 \\ 7 & 0 \end{bmatrix} = \begin{bmatrix} 2+3 & 5+4 \\ -1+7 & 3+0 \end{bmatrix} = \begin{bmatrix} 5 & 9 \\ 6 & 3 \end{bmatrix}$

❏ Two matrices can be added only if they have the same order (that is, the same number of rows and the same number of columns). We can add a 3×2 matrix to another 3×2 matrix, but we cannot add it to a 2×3 or a 4×2 matrix.

❏ A matrix is referred to as a **vector** (it has size and direction). A constant such as the numeral 5 is referred to as a **scalar** (size only).

Whenever a matrix is multiplied by a scalar, each element of the matrix is multiplied by the scalar.

$5 \begin{bmatrix} 4 & 7 \\ -3 & 2 \\ 1 & 5 \end{bmatrix} = \begin{bmatrix} 20 & 35 \\ -15 & 10 \\ 5 & 25 \end{bmatrix}$

❏ $-\mathbf{A}$ is the opposite of $\mathbf{A}$.

A matrix in which every element is zero is called the **zero matrix**.

$\mathbf{A} = \begin{bmatrix} 3 & -1 \\ 4 & 2 \end{bmatrix} \Rightarrow -\mathbf{A} = \begin{bmatrix} -3 & 1 \\ -4 & -2 \end{bmatrix}$

$\mathbf{A} + (-\mathbf{A}) = \begin{bmatrix} 0 & 0 \\ 0 & 0 \end{bmatrix}$

❏ Matrix addition is associative.

If $\mathbf{A} = \begin{bmatrix} 3 & -1 \\ 4 & 2 \end{bmatrix} \quad \mathbf{B} = \begin{bmatrix} 5 & 6 \\ 3 & 1 \end{bmatrix} \quad \mathbf{C} = \begin{bmatrix} -4 & 7 \\ 8 & 3 \end{bmatrix}$

then $(\mathbf{A}+\mathbf{B})+\mathbf{C} = \left[\begin{bmatrix} 3 & -1 \\ 4 & 2 \end{bmatrix} + \begin{bmatrix} 5 & 6 \\ 3 & 1 \end{bmatrix}\right] + \begin{bmatrix} -4 & 7 \\ 8 & 3 \end{bmatrix}$

$= \begin{bmatrix} 8 & 5 \\ 7 & 3 \end{bmatrix} + \begin{bmatrix} -4 & 7 \\ 8 & 3 \end{bmatrix}$

$= \begin{bmatrix} 4 & 12 \\ 15 & 6 \end{bmatrix}$

and $\mathbf{A}+(\mathbf{B}+\mathbf{C}) = \begin{bmatrix} 3 & -1 \\ 4 & 2 \end{bmatrix} + \left[\begin{bmatrix} 5 & 6 \\ 3 & 1 \end{bmatrix} + \begin{bmatrix} -4 & 7 \\ 8 & 3 \end{bmatrix}\right]$

$= \begin{bmatrix} 3 & -1 \\ 4 & 2 \end{bmatrix} + \begin{bmatrix} 1 & 13 \\ 11 & 4 \end{bmatrix}$

$= \begin{bmatrix} 4 & 12 \\ 15 & 6 \end{bmatrix}$

∴ $(\mathbf{A}+\mathbf{B})+\mathbf{C} = \mathbf{A}+(\mathbf{B}+\mathbf{C})$

❏ Matrix addition is commutative.

If $\mathbf{A} = \begin{bmatrix} 3 & -1 \\ 4 & 2 \end{bmatrix}$ $\mathbf{B} = \begin{bmatrix} 5 & 6 \\ 3 & 1 \end{bmatrix}$

then $\mathbf{A}+\mathbf{B} = \begin{bmatrix} 3 & -1 \\ 4 & 2 \end{bmatrix} + \begin{bmatrix} 5 & 6 \\ 3 & 1 \end{bmatrix}$

$= \begin{bmatrix} 8 & 5 \\ 7 & 3 \end{bmatrix}$

and $\mathbf{B}+\mathbf{A} = \begin{bmatrix} 5 & 6 \\ 3 & 1 \end{bmatrix} + \begin{bmatrix} 3 & -1 \\ 4 & 2 \end{bmatrix}$

$= \begin{bmatrix} 8 & 5 \\ 7 & 3 \end{bmatrix}$

∴ $\mathbf{A}+\mathbf{B} = \mathbf{B}+\mathbf{A}$

Translation in the number plane

A point on the number plane is represented by the vector matrix $\begin{bmatrix} x \\ y \end{bmatrix}$.

The point $\begin{bmatrix} x \\ y \end{bmatrix}$ is translated by the vector $\begin{bmatrix} a \\ b \end{bmatrix}$ to the point $\begin{bmatrix} x+a \\ y+b \end{bmatrix}$.

Example:
The point $\begin{bmatrix} 3 \\ -1 \end{bmatrix}$ is translated to $\begin{bmatrix} 7 \\ 2 \end{bmatrix}$ by $\begin{bmatrix} 4 \\ 3 \end{bmatrix}$.

If point A is translated to point B by matrix $\begin{bmatrix} a \\ b \end{bmatrix}$, then the gradient of AB is $\dfrac{b}{a}$.

Multiplication of matrices

❑ When multiplying two matrices, the elements of each column of the second matrix are multiplied by the corresponding elements of each row of the first matrix. These products are added to give the elements of the resulting matrix. The first matrix must have the same number of columns as the second matrix has rows, that is, we can multiply a 2×3 matrix by a 3×2, or a 3×4 matrix.

❑ In general, if we multiply an $m \times n$ matrix by an $n \times p$ matrix the resultant matrix will be $m \times p$.

❑ Multiplying a 2×2 matrix by a 2×1 matrix:
$$\begin{bmatrix} a & b \\ c & d \end{bmatrix} \begin{bmatrix} x \\ y \end{bmatrix} = \begin{bmatrix} ax+by \\ cx+dy \end{bmatrix}$$

Example: $\begin{bmatrix} 5 & 3 \\ 2 & -4 \end{bmatrix} \begin{bmatrix} 7 \\ 1 \end{bmatrix} = \begin{bmatrix} 35+3 \\ 14-4 \end{bmatrix} = \begin{bmatrix} 38 \\ 10 \end{bmatrix}$

❑ Multiplying a 2×2 matrix by a 2×2 matrix:
$$\begin{bmatrix} a & b \\ c & d \end{bmatrix} \begin{bmatrix} w & x \\ y & z \end{bmatrix} = \begin{bmatrix} aw+by & ax+bz \\ cw+dy & cx+dz \end{bmatrix}$$

Example:
$$\begin{bmatrix} 5 & 3 \\ 2 & -4 \end{bmatrix} \begin{bmatrix} 7 & 2 \\ -5 & 6 \end{bmatrix} = \begin{bmatrix} 35-15 & 10+18 \\ 14+20 & 4-24 \end{bmatrix} = \begin{bmatrix} 20 & 28 \\ 34 & -20 \end{bmatrix}$$

- $I = \begin{bmatrix} 1 & 0 \\ 0 & 1 \end{bmatrix}$ is called the **identity matrix**.

  For any matrix **A**, **AI** = **A**.

  If the product of two matrices gives the identity matrix, then the each matrix is the **inverse matrix** of the other. The inverse of **A** is $\mathbf{A}^{-1}$, that is, $\mathbf{AA}^{-1} = \mathbf{I} = \mathbf{A}^{-1}\mathbf{A}$.

- In general, for two matrices **A** and **B**, **AB** ≠ **BA**, that is, multiplication of matrices is *not* commutative.

  If $\quad \mathbf{A} = \begin{bmatrix} 3 & -1 \\ 4 & 2 \end{bmatrix} \quad \mathbf{B} = \begin{bmatrix} 5 & 6 \\ 3 & 1 \end{bmatrix}$

  then, $\quad \mathbf{AB} = \begin{bmatrix} 3 & -1 \\ 4 & 2 \end{bmatrix}\begin{bmatrix} 5 & 6 \\ 3 & 1 \end{bmatrix} = \begin{bmatrix} 12 & 17 \\ 26 & 26 \end{bmatrix}$

  and $\quad \mathbf{BA} = \begin{bmatrix} 5 & 6 \\ 3 & 1 \end{bmatrix}\begin{bmatrix} 3 & -1 \\ 4 & 2 \end{bmatrix} = \begin{bmatrix} 39 & 7 \\ 13 & -1 \end{bmatrix}$

- Matrix multiplication is associative.

  If $\quad \mathbf{A} = \begin{bmatrix} 3 & -1 \\ 4 & 2 \end{bmatrix} \quad \mathbf{B} = \begin{bmatrix} 5 & 6 \\ 3 & 1 \end{bmatrix} \quad \mathbf{C} = \begin{bmatrix} -4 & 7 \\ 8 & 3 \end{bmatrix}$

  then, $(\mathbf{AB})\mathbf{C} = \left[\begin{bmatrix} 3 & -1 \\ 4 & 2 \end{bmatrix}\begin{bmatrix} 5 & 6 \\ 3 & 1 \end{bmatrix}\right]\begin{bmatrix} -4 & 7 \\ 8 & 3 \end{bmatrix}$

  $\quad = \begin{bmatrix} 12 & 17 \\ 26 & 26 \end{bmatrix}\begin{bmatrix} -4 & 7 \\ 8 & 3 \end{bmatrix}$

  $\quad = \begin{bmatrix} 88 & 135 \\ 104 & 260 \end{bmatrix}$

  and $\mathbf{A}(\mathbf{BC}) = \begin{bmatrix} 3 & -1 \\ 4 & 2 \end{bmatrix}\left[\begin{bmatrix} 5 & 6 \\ 3 & 1 \end{bmatrix}\begin{bmatrix} -4 & 7 \\ 8 & 3 \end{bmatrix}\right]$

  $\quad = \begin{bmatrix} 3 & -1 \\ 4 & 2 \end{bmatrix}\begin{bmatrix} 28 & 53 \\ -4 & 24 \end{bmatrix}$

  $\quad = \begin{bmatrix} 88 & 135 \\ 104 & 260 \end{bmatrix}$

  ∴ $(\mathbf{AB})\mathbf{C} = \mathbf{A}(\mathbf{BC})$

Special transformations on the number plane

Matrix	Transformation	Description
$\begin{bmatrix} -1 & 0 \\ 0 & 1 \end{bmatrix}$	$\begin{bmatrix} x \\ y \end{bmatrix} \Rightarrow \begin{bmatrix} -x \\ y \end{bmatrix}$	reflection in the y axis
$\begin{bmatrix} 1 & 0 \\ 0 & -1 \end{bmatrix}$	$\begin{bmatrix} x \\ y \end{bmatrix} \Rightarrow \begin{bmatrix} x \\ -y \end{bmatrix}$	reflection in the x axis
$\begin{bmatrix} 0 & 1 \\ 1 & 0 \end{bmatrix}$	$\begin{bmatrix} x \\ y \end{bmatrix} \Rightarrow \begin{bmatrix} y \\ x \end{bmatrix}$	reflection in the line $y = x$
$\begin{bmatrix} 0 & -1 \\ -1 & 0 \end{bmatrix}$	$\begin{bmatrix} x \\ y \end{bmatrix} \Rightarrow \begin{bmatrix} -y \\ -x \end{bmatrix}$	reflection in the line $y = -x$
$\begin{bmatrix} 0 & -1 \\ 1 & 0 \end{bmatrix}$	$\begin{bmatrix} x \\ y \end{bmatrix} \Rightarrow \begin{bmatrix} -y \\ x \end{bmatrix}$	anti-clockwise rotation of $90°$ about O
$\begin{bmatrix} -1 & 0 \\ 0 & -1 \end{bmatrix}$	$\begin{bmatrix} x \\ y \end{bmatrix} \Rightarrow \begin{bmatrix} -x \\ -y \end{bmatrix}$	rotation of $180°$ about O
$\begin{bmatrix} 0 & 1 \\ -1 & 0 \end{bmatrix}$	$\begin{bmatrix} x \\ y \end{bmatrix} \Rightarrow \begin{bmatrix} y \\ -x \end{bmatrix}$	rotation of $-90°$ (or $270°$) about O
$\begin{bmatrix} k & 0 \\ 0 & k \end{bmatrix}$	$\begin{bmatrix} x \\ y \end{bmatrix} \Rightarrow \begin{bmatrix} kx \\ ky \end{bmatrix}$	enlargement by a factor of k with O as centre of enlargement
$\begin{bmatrix} \frac{1}{k} & 0 \\ 0 & \frac{1}{k} \end{bmatrix}$	$\begin{bmatrix} x \\ y \end{bmatrix} \Rightarrow \begin{bmatrix} \frac{x}{k} \\ \frac{y}{k} \end{bmatrix}$	contraction by a factor of k with O as centre of contraction

Combined transformations

❏ **BA** means transformation **A** followed by transformation **B**.

❏ Multiplying by a matrix **A**, then by matrix **B**, is equivalent to multiplying by the matrix product **BA**.

❏ Two successive reflections are equivalent to one rotation.

❏ Two successive rotations are equivalent to one single rotation.

Chapter 14
SURVEYING

Land surveying is a branch of mathematics which deals with the measuring and recording of the size and shape of a certain section of Earth's surface, and showing this on a map or plan. Surveying is concerned with the measurement of length over the ground.

Principles of surveying

1 Rectangular coordinates

Here the point P is fixed with respect to the survey line AB by the distance QP measured at right-angles to AB from the point Q.

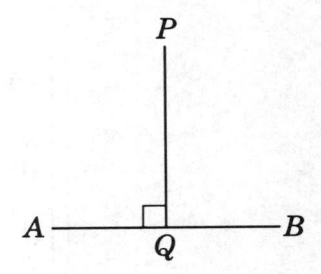

2 Focal coordinates

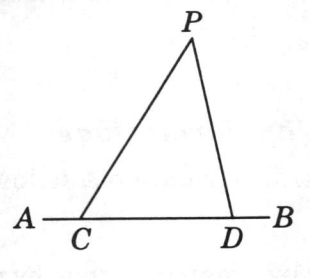

Here the point P is 'tied' by the distances CP and DP, which are measured respectively from C and D, known points on the survey line AB.

3 Angular coordinates

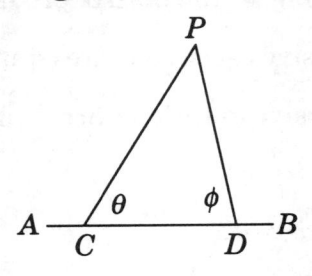

Here the point P is fixed with respect to the survey line AB by the intersection of two visual lines CP and DP, which make observed angles θ and ϕ at known points C and D respectively with line AB.

Note This method is necessary when locating inaccessible points or objects. It is a form of triangulation.

4 Polar coordinates

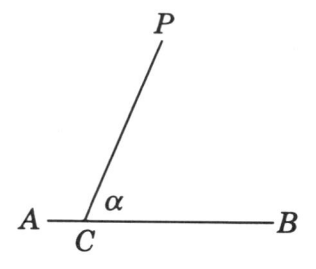

Here the point P is fixed with respect to the survey line AB by the distance CP measured from a known point C at a known angle α to AB.

5 Trilinear coordinates

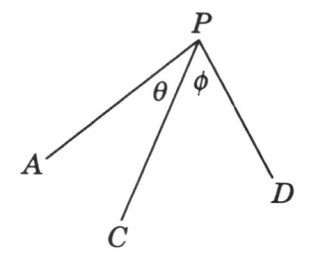

Here the point P is fixed by θ and ϕ, the angles subtended at P by three visible and mapped points A, C, D.

Equipment

The equipment necessary for plane surveying consists of one or two sets of the following:
- ranging rods or pickets
- chain with tellers
- cross-staff or optical square
- field notebook
- theodolite
- flags
- tape measure
- pocket compass
- alidade

Lengths are measured by tape or chain.

Angles are measured by theodolite or alidade.

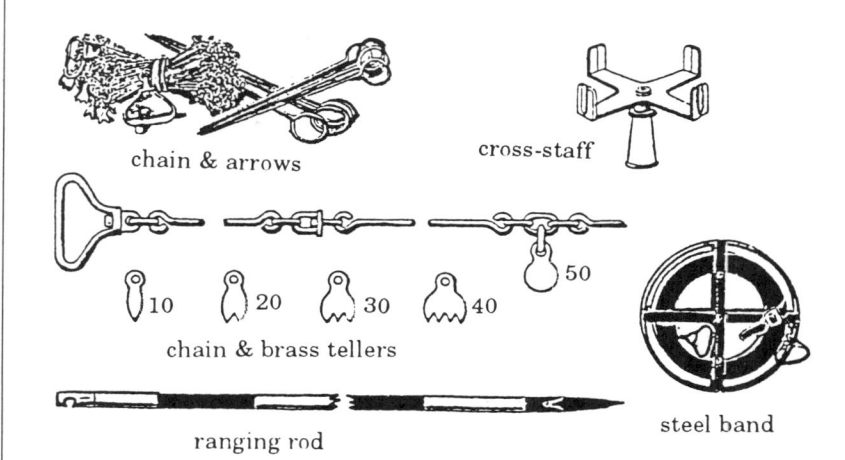

chain & arrows

cross-staff

chain & brass tellers

ranging rod

steel band

Primary surveying methods

Traversing

This denotes the running of consecutive straight survey lines between **stations**.

❑ **Open traverse** consists of a number of survey lines following a particular route and not returning to the starting point.

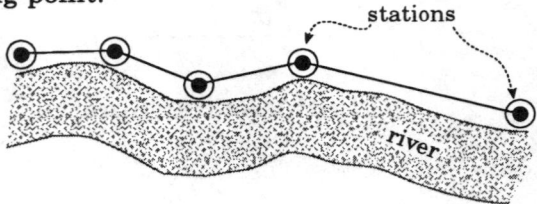

❑ **Closed traverse** consists of a number of survey lines, the last one returning to the starting point, thus forming a closed polygon.

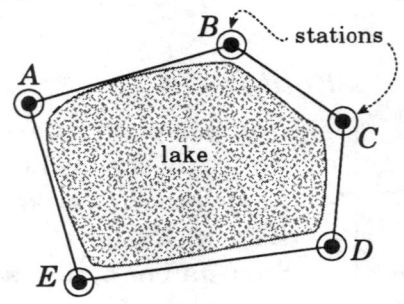

Triangulation

In triangulation the area is covered as completely as possible by a scheme of triangles. From a fixed base line AB we measure angles first from A then from B to each of the stations at $C, D,$ and E. If we know the length of AB, we can calculate all the other sides of the triangles using either the sine rule or the cosine rule.

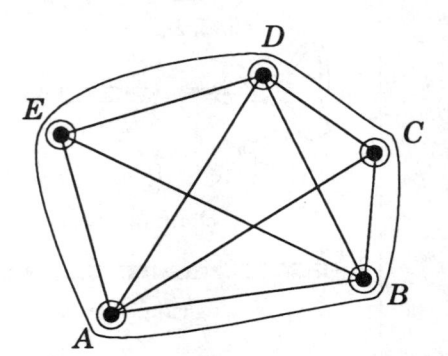

The offset survey

Finding perpendiculars to a line

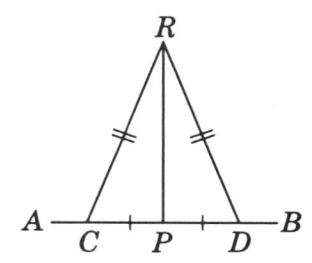

From an internal point P, hold the ends of the tape at points C and D equidistant from P. Stretch out the tape from the middle to fix point R so that $CR = RD$.

Thus, $PR \perp AB$.

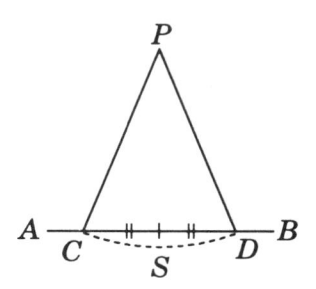

From an external point P, fix the end of the tape at P and swing the tape to cut the line at two points, C and D. Measure the length CD and bisect it at S so that $CS = SD$.

Thus, $PS \perp AB$

The field notebook

	B	
	79	
33	58	
	48	25
27	30	
	0	
	A	

This informs anyone reading the notebook that the survey was taken from A to B with offsets of 27 m and 33 m taken respectively at 30 m, and 58 m from A to the left, and an offset of 25 m was taken to the right at 48 m from A.

The bearing of AB is necessary for correct orientation.

Scale diagrams

Accurate scale diagrams are necessary to measure the perimeter.

For example, use a scale of 1 mm = 1 m (that is, 1 : 1000).

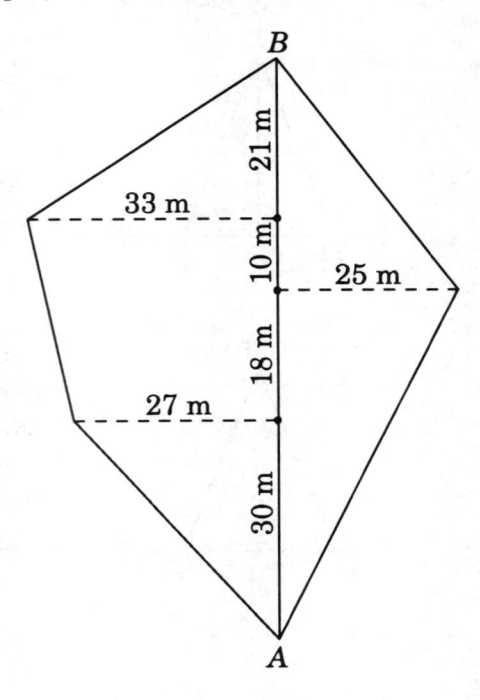

Plane tabling

The plane table may be described as a drawing-board mounted on a tripod to form a table upon which drawing paper is fixed so surveys can be plotted concurrently with the field work, using a sighting device such as an alidade.

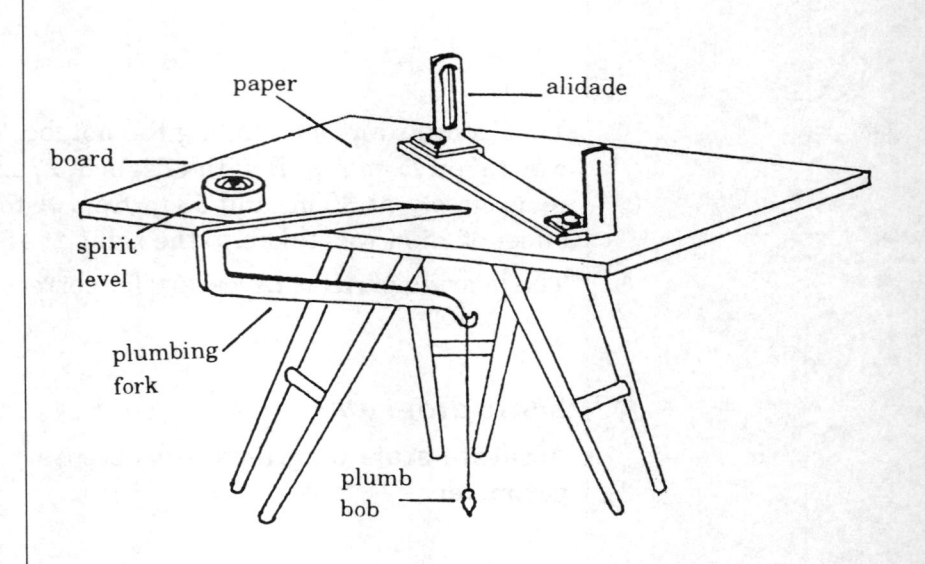

Radial method

This can only be used when all points to be surveyed are accessible.

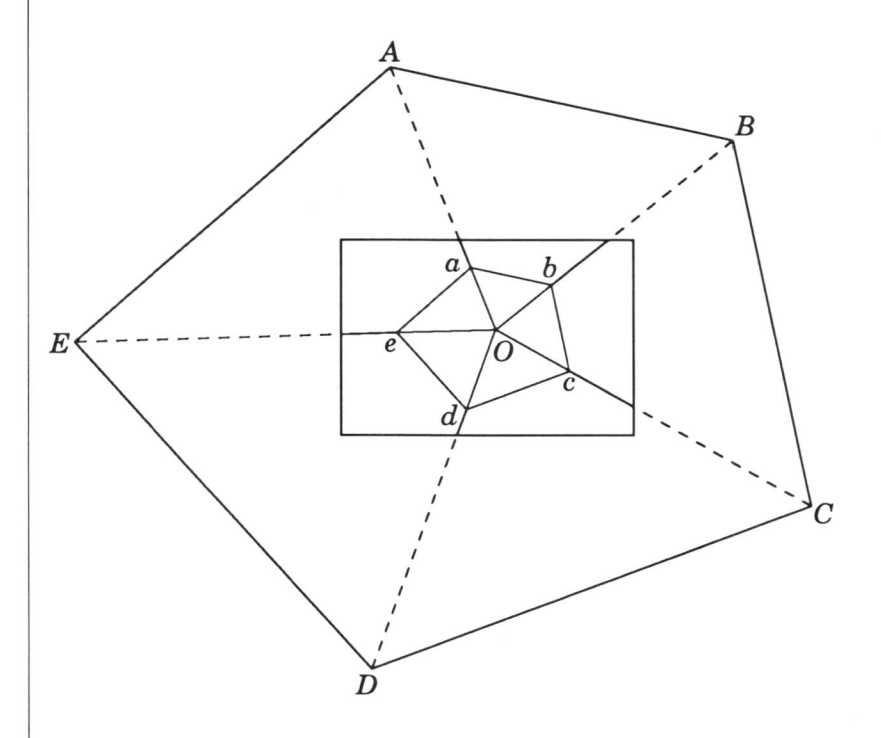

- A station O is selected so that all the points A, B, C, D, E to be surveyed are visible.
- The table is set above this station, marking its position on the drawing sheet by the aid of a plumbing fork.
- Sightings are made towards A, B, C, D, E in turn and their directions are recorded on the drawing sheet.
- The distances OA, OB, OC, OD, OE are obtained by direct measurement using a chain or a tape.
- Their scales Oa, Ob, Oc, Od, Oe are calculated and marked on the drawing sheet.
- The points a, b, c, d, e are connected to obtain the scale drawing of the field.

Example:
A radial survey was carried out using a compass. The bearings and distances are given. Use the information to make a scale drawing and calculate the perimeter and them area of the field.

A is 50 m from O at 060°
B is 90 m from O at 140°
C is 95 m from O at 210°
D is 38 m from O at 310°

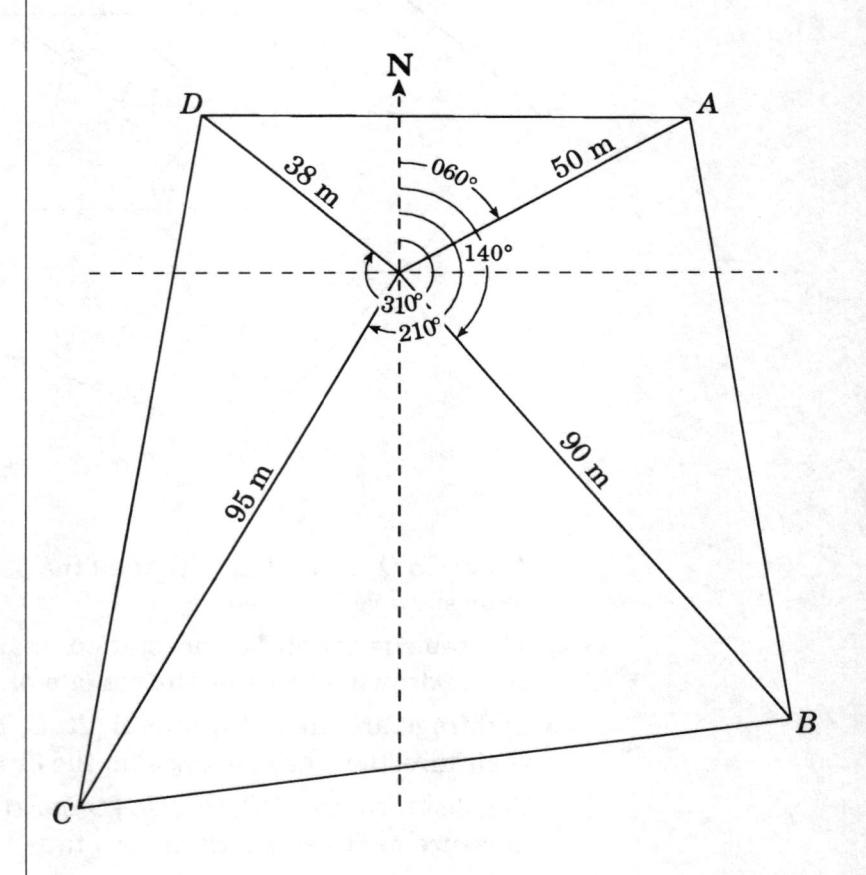

Solution:

Select a suitable scale 1 cm : 20 m

Scale lengths are $OA = 2.5$ cm $OB = 4.5$ cm
 $OC = 4.75$ cm $OD = 1.9$ cm

Perimeter (on drawing) $= AB + BC + CD + DA$
$= 4.9 + 5.4 + 5.3 + 3.6$
$= 19.2$ cm

Perimeter (full size) = 19·2 × 20 m
$$= 384 \text{ m}$$

Area $\angle AOB = 140° - 60° = 80°$
$\angle BOC = 210° - 140° = 70°$
$\angle COD = 310° - 210° = 100°$
$\angle DOA = 60° + 50° = 110°$

Using the formula for the area of a triangle,
area = $\frac{1}{2}ab \sin C$

$\triangle AOB = \frac{1}{2} \times 50 \times 90 \times \sin 80°$
$= 2216 \text{ m}^2$ (to nearest m^2)

$\triangle BOC = \frac{1}{2} \times 90 \times 95 \times \sin 70°$
$= 4017 \text{ m}^2$ (to nearest m^2)

$\triangle COD = \frac{1}{2} \times 95 \times 38 \times \sin 100°$
$= 1778 \text{ m}^2$ (to nearest m^2)

$\triangle DOA = \frac{1}{2} \times 38 \times 50 \times \sin 110°$
$= 893 \text{ m}^2$ (to nearest m^2)

∴   area of $ABCD = 2216 + 4017 + 1778 + 893$
$= 8904 \text{ m}^2.$

Intersection method

Note that this is a form of **triangulation**.

This method is useful when the points to be surveyed are inaccessible.

- The survey line AB is measured directly by a chain or a tape.
- The table is set up above A and a point 'a' is marked on the drawing sheet by the aid of a plumbing fork.
- Sightings are taken towards B, then C, then D and the lines are recorded on the drawing sheet. $\angle DAB$, $\angle CAB$ can be measured using a theodolite, or can be found by measuring the angles on the sheet using a protractor. (It is a good idea to use both for accuracy.)

- ❏ The table is then moved to B and a point 'b' is recorded directly above B on the line from 'a', 'ab' being the scale of AB. The table is oriented so that ab lines up with AB.
- ❏ Sightings are taken towards C, then D and the lines are recorded on the drawing sheet to intersect the previous lines at 'c' and 'd'. $\angle CBA$, $\angle DBA$ can be measured.
- ❏ Finally a, b, c, d are joined to give a scale drawing of the field $ABCD$.
- ❏ The perimeter of the field can be found by:
    - (i) measuring the sides ab, bc, cd, da of the scale drawing and converting it using the scale, or
    - (ii) calculating the lengths of the sides using the sine or cosine rules.

Example:

A triangulation survey was carried out using a compass. AB is a survey line 50 m long. Bearings are taken firstly from A, then B, to points P and Q.

Use the information to make a scale drawing of the field.

Bearing of P from A is 330°
Bearing of P from B is 300°
Bearing of Q from A is 75°
Bearing of Q from B is 20°

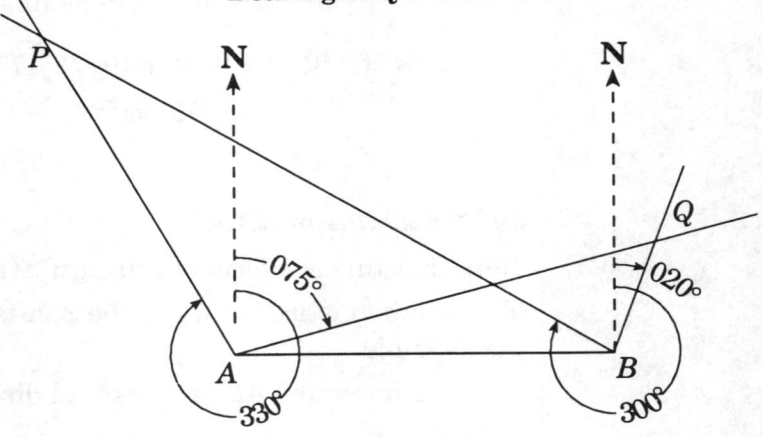

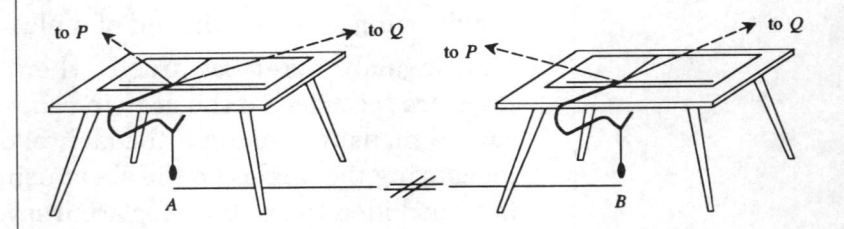

Chapter 15
NAVIGATION

The Earth as a sphere

Great and small circles

If the sphere is cut by a flat plane, a **circle** is formed on the surface of the sphere.

If this plane passes through the centre of the sphere, then a **great circle** is formed.

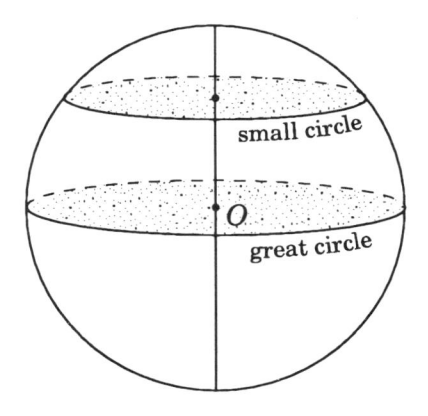

The axis and the equator

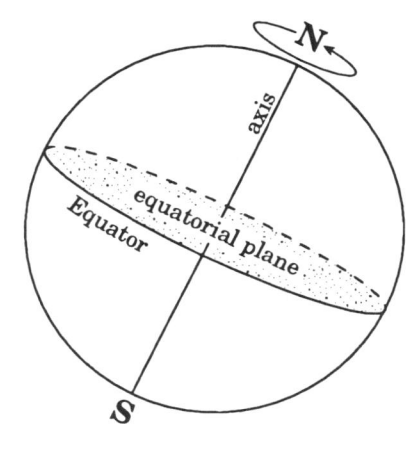

Any line through the centre of a sphere is a **diameter**.

The diameter of Earth passing through the North and South poles is called the **axis**.

The plane, ⊥ to the axis and passing through the centre of Earth, is called the **Equator**.

Latitude and longitude

Circles parallel to the Equator are small circles called **parallels of latitude**.

The latitude of a point is the angular distance of the point north or south of the Equator.

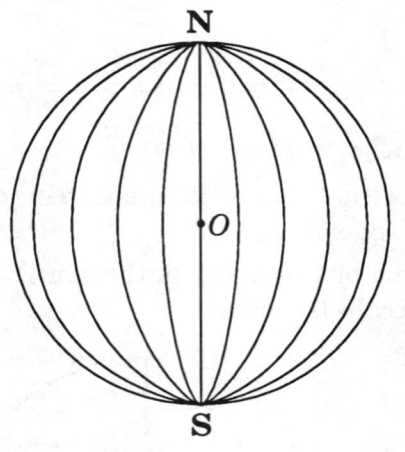

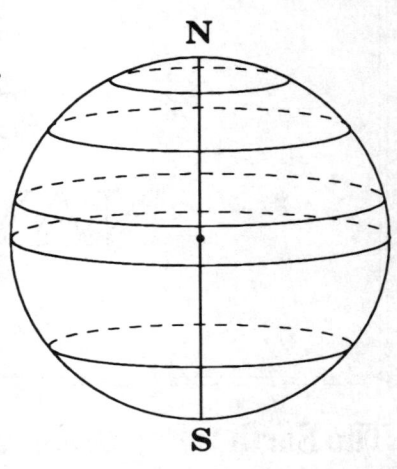

Earth is cut by imaginary great circles passing through the North and South poles into wedges. The poles divide each into semicircles called **meridians of longitude**.

The longitude of a point is the angular distance of the point east or west of the prime (or Greenwich) meridian.

Example: A is (60°N, 20°W)
B is (30°N, 20°W)
C is (0°, 20°W)
D is (60°N, 0°)
E is (30°N, 40°E)
F is (30°S, 40°E)
G is (0°, 0°)

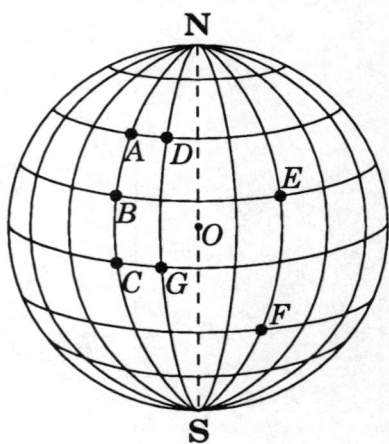

Longitude and time

True noon for any place is the instant when the sun is at its highest point in the sky; that is, when the sun is directly over all the points on that meridian.

All points on the same meridian have the same true noon, and, theoretically, the same local time, although adjustments such as daylight saving are often made.

A difference in longitude of 15° between two places on Earth means a difference of 1 hour in the local times for these places.

NAVIGATION

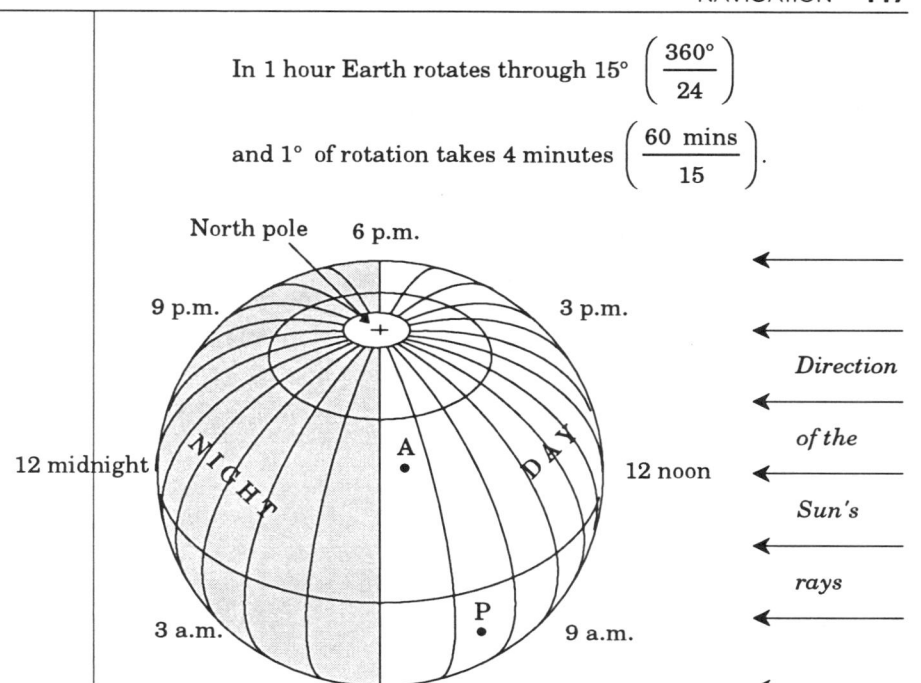

In 1 hour Earth rotates through 15° $\left(\dfrac{360°}{24}\right)$

and 1° of rotation takes 4 minutes $\left(\dfrac{60 \text{ mins}}{15}\right)$.

Earth at the Autumnal Equinox (22 September)

Since P is **EAST** of A, P is **AHEAD** of A in local time.

Standard time

For convenience, certain countries have instituted **standard time zones**.

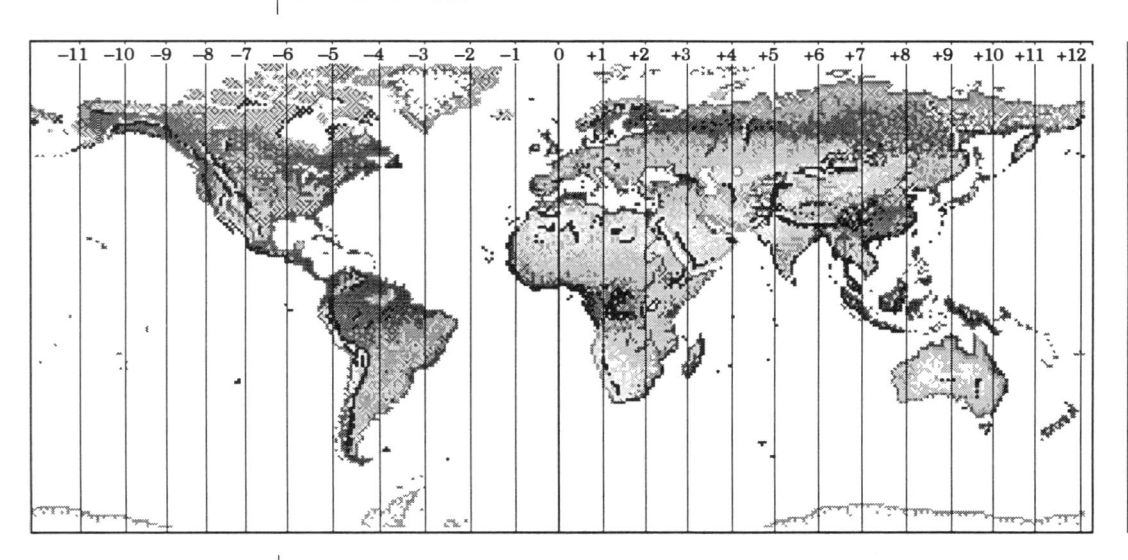

Charts

Mercator's projection

- Meridians appear as equally spaced parallel lines.
- Parallels of latitude are unequally spaced, spacing increasing further from the Equator and appearing perpendicular to meridians.
- Any straight line on the chart is a line of **constant bearing** (that is, a line which crosses all meridians at the same angle). In navigation, the line of constant bearing is called a **rhumb line**.
- Measuring of distances is simplified by the use of **latitude scales**.

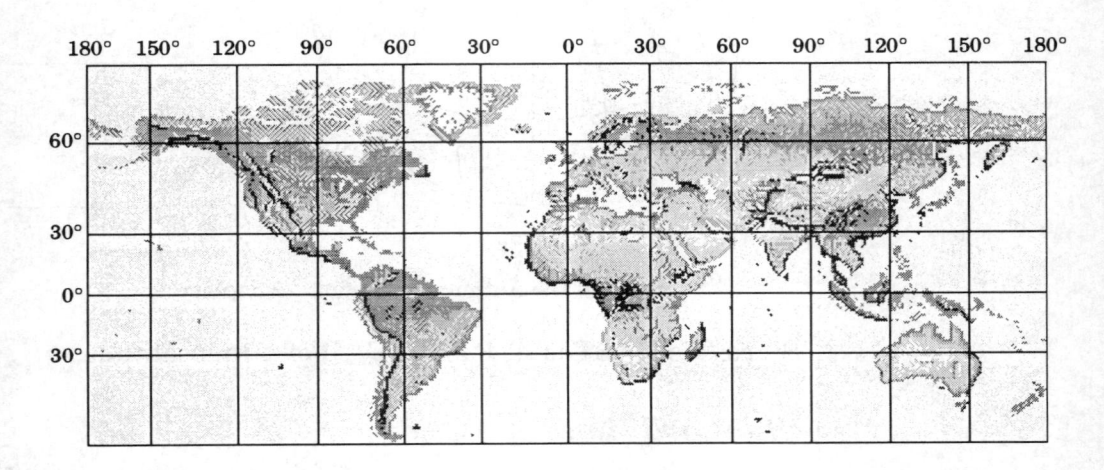

Distances using the latitude scale

- The **international nautical mile** is defined to be exactly 1852 metres.

    Previously a nautical mile was defined as the length of an arc of a great circle subtended by an angle of 1 minute at the centre of Earth, and this is used for convenience.

    Thus, on a chart, a distance of one nautical mile is one minute on the latitude scale.

    1 minute of latitude = 1 nautical mile
    (measured on a great circle)

- The **knot** is the speed with which a vessel moves through the water.

    1 knot = 1 nautical mile per hour

NAVIGATION

Direction

❏ A **bearing** is the angular direction from one point to another.

The **true bearing** is always measured from north in a clockwise direction. It is always given as a 3-digit angle, taking values from 000° up to but not including 360°.

For example, the bearing of *A* from *O* is 125°T.

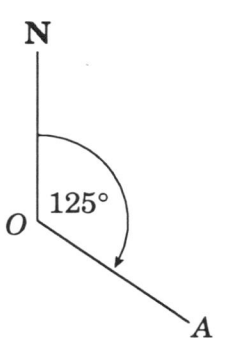

❏ A **magnetic compass** uses a magnetic needle which always points to the magnetic North Pole.

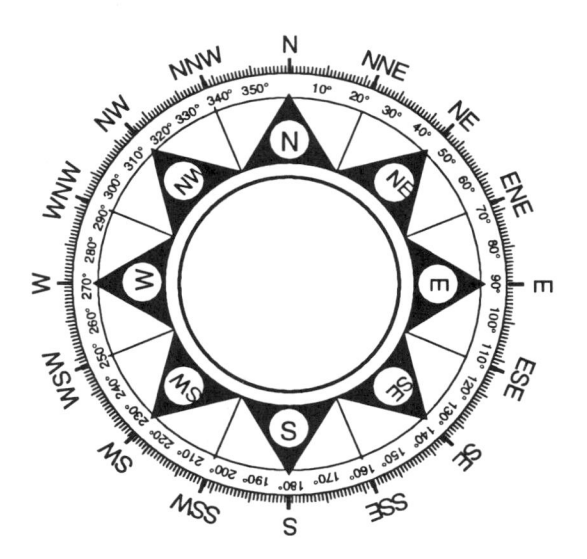

Variation

Magnetic north does not coincide with true north. The magnetic North Pole lies in the north-eastern corner of Canada.

The angular distance between the magnetic North Pole and the geographic North Pole is known as **variation**.

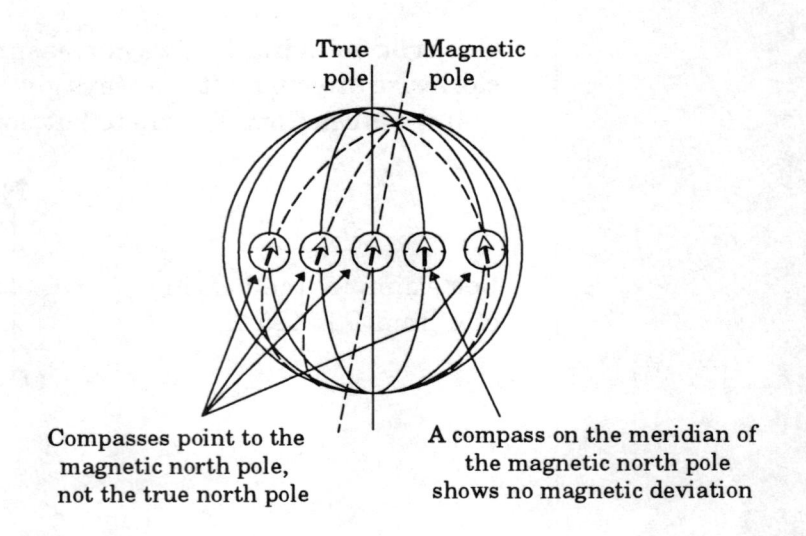

True pole | Magnetic pole

Compasses point to the magnetic north pole, not the true north pole

A compass on the meridian of the magnetic north pole shows no magnetic deviation

A **compass rose** is present on all navigation charts. It is aligned with the geographic North Pole. The variation is clearly indicated.

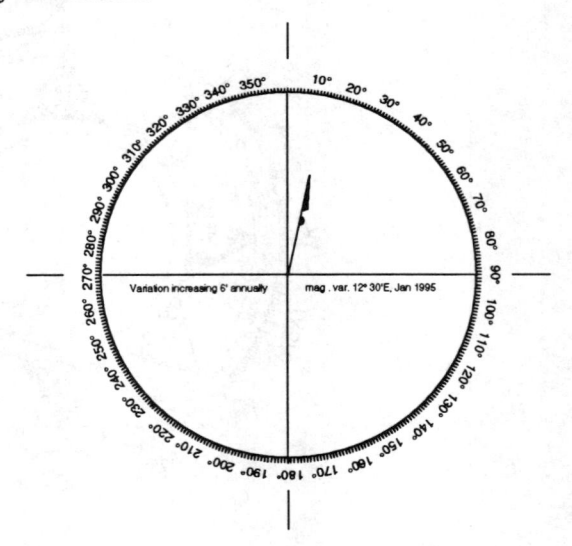

Variation increasing 6' annually   mag . var. 12° 30'E, Jan 1995

If the variation is east,
    true bearing = compass bearing + variation

If the variation is west,
    true bearing = compass bearing − variation

There is a useful *rule of thumb* for calculating a compass course:

**ERROR EAST, COMPASS LEAST
ERROR WEST, COMPASS BEST.**

Examples:
- **(a)** True course   220° T
  Compass error   12° E
  Compass course   208° C   (error east, compass least)
- **(b)** True course   120° T
  Compass error   10° W
  Compass course   130° C   (error west, compass best)

Fixing positions

Two-transit fix

Any two fixed objects on the shore can give a line of bearing called a **transit**. If two such transits cross, a **fix** is found.

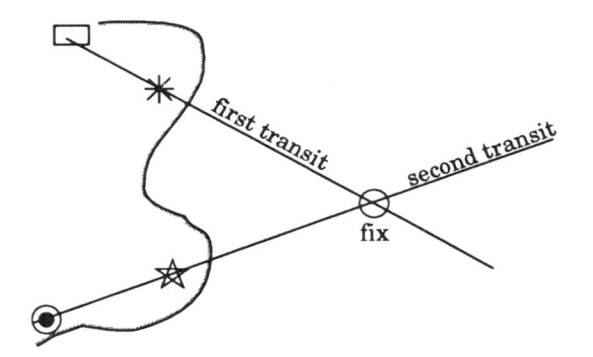

Cross-bearing fix

Bearings are taken in quick succession of two or more shore objects which are easily identified on the chart. It is best done with three objects spaced out so that the angle between adjacent objects is not be less than 30°.

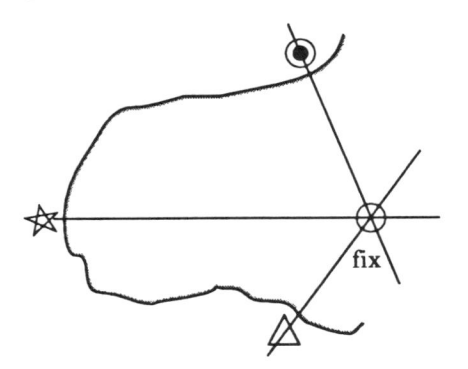

Often, due to small errors in observation, the three position lines do not intersect exactly, forming a small triangle. This is known as a **cocked hat**.

A small cocked hat can be accepted, taking the corner of the triangle closest to shore as the fix.

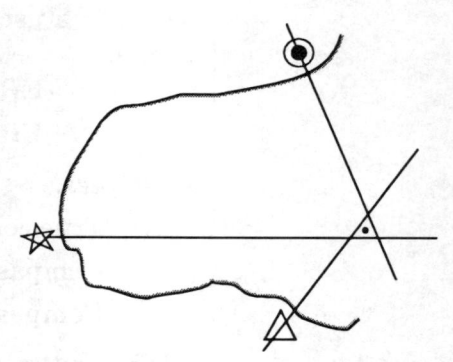

A large cocked hat indicates that the fix should be redone or discarded.

Vertical angle and compass fix

For a vertical angle fix we need an object on shore, the height of which is known. A lighthouse is generally useful for this. The angle of elevation of the object is measured from the boat using a sextant.

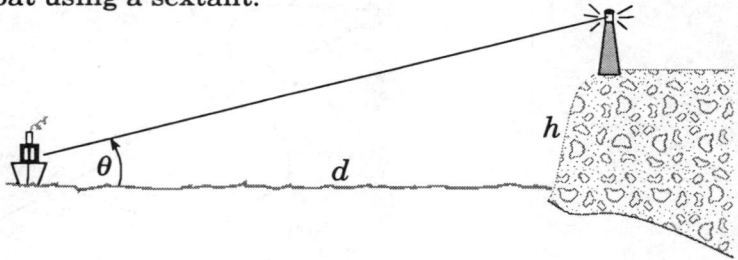

To find the distance from a lighthouse use the formula:

$$d = \frac{h}{\tan \theta \times 1852}$$

$\begin{cases} h = \text{height of lighthouse in metres} \\ \theta = \text{angle of elevation} \\ d = \text{distance in nautical miles} \end{cases}$

Example:

Find the distance of a boat from shore if the angle of elevation of a lighthouse 120 m above sea-level is 2° 10'.

$$d = \frac{120}{\tan 2° 10' \times 1852}$$

$$= 1.71 \text{ nautical miles}$$

Plotting a course

When a course is plotted on a chart it is called a **sea plot**. A sea plot is always commenced with a **fix**.

Chapter 16
LINEAR PROGRAMMING

A **linear program** is a method of deciding on the best course of action in planning and strategy in industry, commerce and national defence.

The vital factors are expressed in mathematical language as linear inequalities called **constraints**.

Theorem

A linear expression, $Ax + By + C$, evaluated at points of a convex polygonal region defined by a system of linear inequalities takes on its maximum and minimum values at corner points.

Example:

A farmer has 120 hectares which he could use for planting. He can afford to spend $800 on seed, and up to $8400 on labour. He decides to grow two crops, wheat and corn, though he does not know how many hectares of each he should plant in order to obtain the maximum profit. He has a fixed order with the local produce store to supply them with the yield of 10 hectares of corn. Wheat costs $10 per hectare for seed, $24 per hectare for labour and gives a gross return of $114 per hectare. Corn gives a gross return of $176 per hectare, but seed costs $4 and labour costs $72 per hectare.

Solution:
Let the number of hectares of wheat be x and the number of hectares of corn be y.

$$\text{Gross receipts} = \$(114x + 176y)$$
$$\text{Total expenses} = \$(34x + 76y)$$
$$\text{Profit} = \$(80x + 100y)$$

Thus in this case we wish to find an ordered pair (x, y) such that $80x + 100y$ is a maximum.

Expressing each constraint as an inequality:

1. The farmer can use at most 120 hectares.
$$x + y \le 120$$

2. He must produce 10 hectares of corn for the store.
$$y \ge 10$$

3. The least possible number of hectares of wheat is 0.
$$x \ge 0$$

4. He can afford at most $800 for seed.
$$10x + 4y \le 800$$
that is, $5x + 2y \le 400$

5. He can afford at most $8400 for labour.
$$24x + 72y \le 8400$$
that is, $x + 3y \le 350$

In summary, we have to maximise the linear expression $80x + 100y$ subject to the 5 constraints

$$x + y \le 120$$
$$y \ge 10$$
$$x \ge 0$$
$$5x + 2y \le 400$$
$$x + 3y \le 350$$

In other words we wish to find an ordered pair (x, y) satisfying each of the 5 inequalities, which will make the linear expression $80x + 100y$ as large as possible.

Graphing the inequalities, we get:

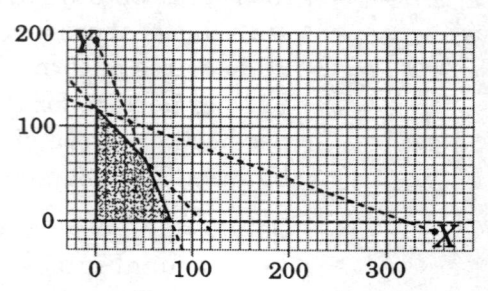

The corner points of the polygon obtained by solving the various pairs of linear equations are

$(0, 10)$, $\left(0, 116\frac{2}{3}\right)$, $(5, 115)$, $\left(53\frac{1}{3}, 66\frac{2}{3}\right)$, $(76, 10)$.

To solve the farmer's problem we substitute each ordered pair into the linear expression $80x + 100y$ to see which pair gives the greatest value.

On substitution $(5, 115)$ gives the greatest profit of $11 900.

Chapter 17
SET THEORY

In mathematics a collection of things is called a **set**. An object belonging to a set is called an **element** or **member** of the set. In a set each element is listed *once* only.

Methods of describing sets
- ❑ By listing the elements in braces, for example, {a, b, c, d}
- ❑ By describing the condition for membership in the set. For example, the set of the first four letters of the alphabet.

Symbols

{ }	set
∈	is an element of
∉	is not an element of
∪	union
∩	intersection
⊂	is a subset of
⊄	is not a subset of
∅ or { }	empty set
↔	equivalent (sets)
n( )	number of elements

If $A = \{2, 3, 5, 7, 11, 13, 17, 19\}$,

then $2 \in A$, $8 \notin A$, $\{2, 3, 5, 7\} \subset A$.

Equivalent sets

Two sets are equivalent if their elements can be matched one-to-one, that is, they contain the same number of elements.

$$A = \{©, ®, @, ⊗, ⊕\}$$
$$\updownarrow \;\; \updownarrow \;\; \updownarrow \;\; \updownarrow \;\; \updownarrow$$
$$B = \{♠, ♥, ♦, ♣, ✽\}$$

A is equivalent to B since $n(A) = n(B) = 5$, that is, $A \leftrightarrow B$.

Finite, infinite and empty sets

- The set of letters of the alphabet is **finite**, because the number of elements can be counted.
- The set of elements of all counting numbers is **infinite**, because we cannot count them all.
- The set of cars which may be registered with only one wheel is an **empty set** ($\emptyset$), because there are no such cars.

Subsets

If $A = \{1, 2, 3, 4, 5, 6, 7, 8, 9, 10\}$ and $B = \{2, 4, 6, 8\}$, then $B \subset A$, that is, B is a subset of A, since all elements of B are also elements of A.

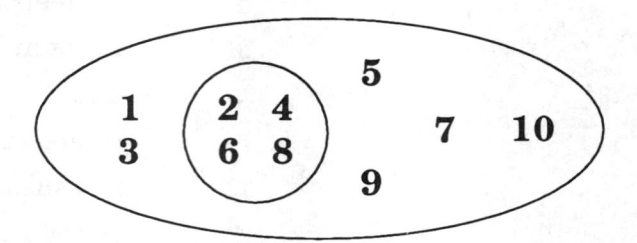

The Venn diagram

A Venn diagram is a pictorial representation of the relationship between sets.

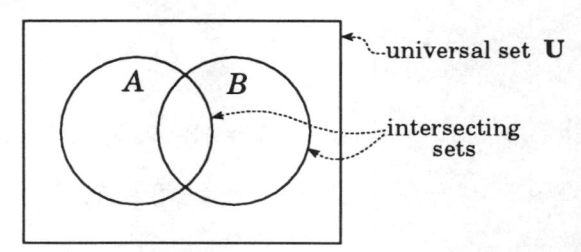

The sets are represented by **simple closed curves,** usually circles.

The universal set **U** is represented by a rectangle enclosing all the circles.

Union and intersection of sets

❑ The **union** of two sets is obtained by writing down all the elements of the first set and then including all the elements of the second set **not already** included.

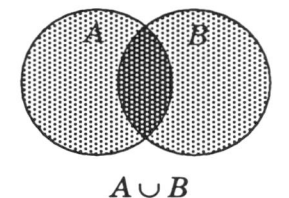

$A \cup B$

❑ The intersection of two sets is obtained by writing down all the elements **common** to the two sets.

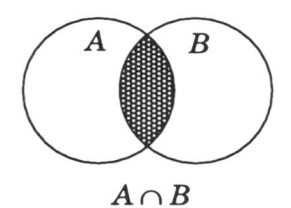

$A \cap B$

Example: $A = \{1, 2, 3, 4, 5, 6, 7, 8, 9\}$

$B = \{4, 8, 12, 16\}$

The union of A and B is $\{1, 2, 3, 4, 5, 6, 7, 8, 9, 12, 16\}$, and is written

$$A \cup B = \{1, 2, 3, 4, 5, 6, 7, 8, 9, 12, 16\}.$$

The intersection of A and B is $\{4, 8\}$, and is written,

$$A \cap B = \{4, 8\}.$$

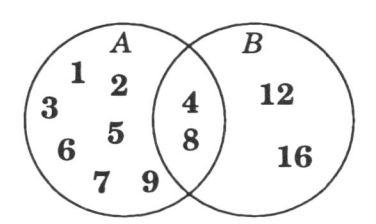

INDEX

a

acute angles 33
adding and subtracting
    algebraic fractions 20
    decimals 6
    directed numbers 4
    fractions 5
    matrices 101
    polynomials 96
adjacent angles 33, 34
algebra 16–27
    abbreviations 17
algebraic fractions 20
alternate angles 35
alternate segment theorem 48
angle construction
    of 60° 40
    of right angles 40
angle sum
    of a quadrilateral 38
    of a triangle 37
angle theorems 36–9
    of the circle 46
angles 33–5
    alternate 35
    at a point 36
    bisecting 39
    cointerior 35
    complementary 34
    copying 40
    corresponding 35
    of depression 75
    of elevation 75
    and lines cut by a transversal 35
    measuring 34
    naming 33
    of parallel lines 37
    supplementary 34
    types of 33
    vertically opposite 36
angular coordinates 106
arc, of circle 31
area 52
    of composite figures 55
    formulas 53–4
    of a triangle 53, 78
axis of the Earth 115
axis of symmetry 29

b

bearings 119
binomial products 18
bisecting angles 39
bisecting intervals 39
box-and-whisker plots 65

c

capacity 53
cardinal numbers 9

centre of symmetry 30
charts 118–20
chord 31
   theorems of the circle 47
circles
   area 54
   angle theorems of 46
   chord theorems of 47
   circumference (perimeter) 54
   geometry 45–8
   parts of 31
   properties of 45
   tangent theorems of 47
cointerior angles 35
column graphs 57
common factors 10
   and algebra 18
compass rose 120
compasses, using 51
complementary angles 34
completing the square 27
composite figures, formulas 55
composite functions 90
composite mappings 89
composite numbers 10
compound interest 69–70
cones 32
   surface area 54
   volume 53, 54
congruent triangles 41–2, 44
conjugates 22
constant bearings 118
constants 16
constructions with ruler and compass 39–41
consumer arithmetic 69–72
conversion graphs 81
coordinate geometry 79–85
coordinates of a point 79

corresponding angles 35
cosine (cos) 73, 75–6
cosine rule 77–8
counting numbers 9
cross-bearing fix 121
cross-section 31
cube, surface area and volume 54
cube roots 11
cumulative frequency 60
cylinders 32
   surface area 52
   volume 52

d

decagon 29
decimals 7
   adding and subtracting 7
   converting to percentages and fractions 8
   multiplying and dividing 7
   recurring 12
   rounding 7
denominators 4
dependent variables 16
depreciation 70
deviations from the mean 61
diameter 31
difference of two squares 18
directed numbers 4
distance between two points 82
distribution tables 60
divisibility tests 11–12
domain 86–7
dot plots 57

e

Earth as a sphere 115–17
edge of a shape 31

ellipse 29
empty sets 126
equally likely outcomes 67
equations
    exponential 92
    linear 83–4
    simultaneous 26
    solving 23–4
equations of straight lines 83–4
    general form 83
    gradient–intercept form 83
    point–gradient form 83
    two-point form 83
Equator 115
equilateral triangles 38
equivalent fractions 5
equivalent sets 126
even numbers 9
expanded notation 2
experimental probability 66
exponential equations 92
exponential graphs 92–3
exterior angle of a triangle 38

f

face of a solid 31
factor theorem 97–8
factorising 18–20
    solving quadratic equations 27
factors 9–10
field notebook 109
finite sets 126
fixing positions 121–2
focal coordinates 106
formulas 25–6
    changing the subject 26
    constructing 25
    for mensuration 53–5

fractions 4–5
    adding and subtracting 5
    algebraic 20
    converting to percentages and decimals 8
    multiplying and dividing 6
frequency 60
frequency histograms 58–9
frequency polygons 58–9
functions 86–91
    notation 87
    vertical line test 86

g

geometry 28–48
gradient 82
    and equations of straight lines 83–4
    of parallel lines 84
    of perpendicular lines 84
graphs
    of curves 81
    of lines 80
    of inequations 24–5
    of polynomial functions 98–9
    logarithmic and exponential 92–3
    statistical 56–9
great circles 115
grid diagrams 68
grouping symbols
    and order of operations 2
    removing 18
grouping terms, and factorising 19

h

heptagon 28
hexagon 28
highest common factor (HCF) 10–11
Hindu–Arabic numerals 1

INDEX **131**

hire purchase 71
histograms 58–9
home loans 71–2
hyperbolas 81
hypotenuse 35

i

identity mapping 90
identity matrix 104
improper fractions 4
independent variables 16
index laws 23
indices 22–3
   powers of 23
inequations, graphing on the number line 24–5
infinite sets 126
integers 9
interest 69–70
interquartile range 64
intersection of sets 127
inverse functions 90–1
inverse matrix 104
irrational numbers 13
isosceles triangles 28, 38

k

kites 29
   perimeter and area 54
knots 118

l

latitude 116
   scales 118
laws
   of indices 23
   of logarithms 93–4
   of surds 20–1
LCD 5
LCM 11
like terms 17
   grouping 19
line graphs 58, 80
line symmetry 29
linear equations *see* equations of straight lines
linear programming 123–4
logarithmic graphs 92–3
logarithms 92–4
   definition 92
   laws of 93–4
longitude 116
   and time 116–17
lowest common denominator (LCD) 5
lowest common multiple (LCM) 11

m

mapping of functions 87–8
   composite 89
   identity 90
   two variable 88
mass 53
mathematical language 3
matrices 100–5
   addition of 101
   definitions 100
   multiplication of 103–4
   special transformations in the number plane 105
mean 61
   deviation from 61
mean deviation 62
measurement 49–55
   units and symbols 49–50
measures of central tendency 61
measuring instruments 50–1

median 61
mensuration 52–5
   formulas 53–5
Mercator's projection 118
meridians of longitude 116
midpoint of an interval 81
mixed numbers 4
   adding and subtracting 5–6
   multiplying and dividing 6
mode 61
monic trinomials 18
multiples 9–10
multiplying matrices 103–4
multiplying and dividing
   algebraic fractions 20
   decimals 7
   directed numbers 4
   fractions 5
   indices 22–3
   polynomials 96–7

n

natural numbers 9
nautical mile 118
navigation 115–22
nets of solids 33
nonagon 29
normal distribution 63
number lines 4
   graphing inequations 24–5
number plane 79–81
   plotting points 79
   special transformations of
      matrices in 105
   and translation of matrices 102–3
number properties 2–3
number theory 9–12
numbers and digits 1
numerators 4

o

obtuse angles 33
octagons 29
odd numbers 9
offset survey 109
order of symmetry 30
order of operations 2
ordered pairs 79
ordinal numbers 9

p

parabolas 81
parallel lines
   angles of 37
   constructing 40
   equations of 84
parallelogram 28
   perimeter and area 53
pentagons 28
percentage composition 8
percentages 7–8
   converting to decimals and
      fractions 8
perfect squares 18
   factorising 19
perigon angle 33
perimeter 52
   of composite figures 55
   formulas 53–4
perpendicular lines
   constructing 41
   equations of 84–5
picture graphs 56
pie charts 56
place value 1
plane shapes 28–31
plane tabling 110–14
   intersection method 113–14

radial method 111–13
plotting points on the number plane 79
plotting a course 122
point symmetry 30
polar coordinates 107
polygons 28–9
polynomials 95–9
    addition and subtraction 96
    definition 95
    graphs of 98–9
    multiplication and division 96–7
    notation 95
powers of indices 23
prime factors 10
prime numbers 10
prisms 31, 32
    surface area 54
    volume 52, 54
probability 66–8
    definition of 66, 67
    experimental 66
    range of 67
    theoretical 66–7
pronumerals 16
proper fractions 4
protractors 34, 51
pyramids 32
    surface area 54, 55
    volume 53, 54, 55
Pythagoras' theorem 35–6

q

quadratic equations
    solving by completing the square 27
    solving by factorisation 27
    solving by the quadratic formula 27
quadratic formula 27
quadratic surds 20–2
    rationalising the denominator 21
quadrilaterals, properties of 44–5
    angle sum of 38

r

radius 31
random experiments 66
random variables 59
range
    of data 61
    of a function or relation 86–7
rates 14
    conversions 14
rational numbers 12
ratios 13–14
    division of quantities into 13
    equivalent 13
    and scale drawing 14
rectangle 28
    perimeter and area 53
rectangular coordinates 106
recurring decimals 12
reflection
    of functions 89
    of plane shapes 29
reflex angles 33
relations 86
relative frequency 60
    and experimental probability 66
remainder theorem 97
revolution angle 33
rhombus 28
    perimeter and area 53
rhumb line 118
right-angled triangle 28
right angles 33
    constructing 40
Roman numerals 1
roots, square and cube 11

rotational symmetry 30
rotations
   of functions 89
   of plane shapes 29
rounding 6
rulers 5

S

sample space 67
scale drawing 14
   and surveying 109–10
scalene triangles 28
scientific notation 15
secant, of circle 31
sector, of circle 31
segment, of circle 31
set squares 51
set theory 125–7
significant figures 7
similar triangles 43
simple fractions 4
simple interest 69
simplifying algebraic expressions 17
simultaneous equations
   solving by elimination 26
   solving by substitution 26
sine (sin) 73, 75–6
sine rule 76–7
small circles 115
solid shapes 31–3
solving equations 23–4
   one-step 23
   quadratic 27
   simultaneous 26
   two-step 23
   three-step 24
spheres 32
   surface area 55

volume 55
square 28
   perimeter and area 53
square matrices 100
square numbers 9
square roots 11
standard deviation 62
   uses of 63–5
standard time zones 117
statistics 56–65
stem-and-leaf plots 57–8
straight angles 33
straight lines, equations of 83–4
subsets 126
substitution 16–17
   solving simultaneous equations 26
supplementary angles 34
surds, laws of 20–1
surface area 53
   of composite figures 55
   formulas 54–5
surveying 106–14
   equipment 107
   methods 108
   principles of 106
symbols
   set theory 125
   mathematical 3
   of measurement 46
   for theorems 36
symmetric matrices 100
symmetry 29–30

T

tangent of circle 31
   theorems 47
tangent (tan) 73, 75–6
theoretical probability 66–7

time
    and calendar 50
    and longitude 116–17
    standard zones 117
transformations
    of functions 88–90
    of matrices 105
    of plane shapes 29
translations
    of functions 88
    of matrices 102–3
    of plane shapes 29
transversals and angles 35
trapezium 28
    perimeter and area 53
travel graphs 80
traversing 108
tree diagrams 67
triangle area, and trigonometry 78
triangles
    angle sum of 37
    area 53, 78
    congruent 41–2
    equilateral 28, 38
    exterior angle of 38
    isosceles 28, 38
    perimeter of 53
    right-angled 28
    scalene 28
    similar 43
    solving trigonometrically 74
triangular numbers 9
triangulation 108

trigonometric ratios
    definitions 73
    as coordinates of a point on the unit circle 75–6
trigonometry 73–8
trilinear coordinates 107
trinomials, factorising 18–19
true bearings 119
two-transit fix 121

U

union of sets 127
units of measurement 49–50
unlike terms 17

V

variables 16
variance 62
variation, compass 119–20
Venn diagrams 126–7
vertex 31
vertical angle and compass fix 122
vertical line test for functions 86
vertically opposite angles 36
volume 52–3
    of composite figures 55
    formulas 54–5

Z

zero matrix 101